D0460080

Relating to People
of Other Religions

Relating to People of Other Religions

What Every Christian Needs to Know

M. Thomas Thangaraj

Abingdon Press / Nashville

RELATING TO PEOPLE OF OTHER RELIGIONS
WHAT EVERY CHRISTIAN NEEDS TO KNOW

Copyright © 1997 by Abingdon Press

All rights reserved.
No part of this work may be reproduced or transmitted in any form or by any means, electronic or mechanical, including photocopying and recording, or by any information storage or retrieval system, except as may be expressly permitted by the 1976 Copyright Act or in writing from the publisher. Requests for permission should be addressed to Abingdon Press, P.O. Box 801, 201 Eighth Avenue South, Nashville, TN 37202-0801.

This book is printed on recycled, acid-free, elemental-chlorine-free paper.

0-687-05139-8

ISBN 13: 978-0-687-05139-7

Scripture quotations are from the New Revised Standard Version Bible, copyright © 1989, by the Division of Christian Education of the National Council of the Churches of Christ in the United States of America.

The quotation on p. 29 is from the hymn "God of Many Names," by Brian Wren. Words © 1986 by Hope Publishing Co., Carol Stream, IL 60188. All rights reserved. Used by permission.

07 08 09 10 11—13 12 11 10 9

MANUFACTURED IN THE UNITED STATES OF AMERICA

Contents

CHAPTER 1

My New Neighbor

Ganga and I are fellow pilgrims on the journey of faith. He is a Hindu who teaches Hindu philosophy at a university in Madurai, South India. He also teaches Hinduism to students preparing for Christian ministry at a seminary in the same town. Several times I have gone to the Hindu temple with Ganga. After walking through the outer corridors of the temple and arriving at the inner sanctuary, we would be greeted by a big sign that read, "Only Hindus allowed beyond this point!" This sign was put up recently in response to the insensitive and irreverent behavior of some non-Hindu tourists. Every time we went, Ganga chose not to go into the inner sanctuary lest I feel discriminated against; instead, he would stand at the entrance to the inner sanctuary for a moment, then fall on the floor facing the image of the goddess and pray.

While I stood there next to him lying on the floor, I found myself flooded with questions: Should I also say a prayer silently? Can I pray to the goddess in the sanctuary? Is it even possible to pray to God in this place? If I do pray, will I be compromising my Christian faith? Being Christian, I did not perceive God in the figure of the goddess, because my picture of God has been shaped by the figure of Christ. In that sense, then, I could not pray to God in that setting. But at the same time, Ganga's graciousness in not leaving me alone by going into the sanctuary, the genuineness of his piety and devotion, and his companionship in my faith journey made God's presence very real to me as I stood in that temple. Most often, then, I would close my eyes and say this prayer silently: "God, I thank you for Ganga, a brother in faith, whom you have given me!" That is all I could do.

My visits to the Hindu temple were wrought with dilemmas and questions, but Ganga had a different experience. While he was a visiting scholar at an American university, he attended a nearby Methodist church every Sunday, participating in all the elements of the liturgy, including the Eucharist. When I asked him how he could do this, he told me that he felt as much at home in a Christian church as he would in a Hindu temple. Since there were no Hindu temples nearby, the Methodist church offered him the sacred space he needed to worship God. I marvel at this quite often. How can my Hindu friend worship God easily in a Christian setting, while I have so much difficulty doing the same in a Hindu temple? When I consider this problem carefully, it becomes clear that the ideas and practices that shaped my religious devotion are very different from those that shaped Ganga's. My religious experience has produced an approach to other religious traditions that makes it difficult for me to pray with my Hindu friend and in a Hindu setting of worship.

What is it about my Christian upbringing that creates barriers to relating to people of other religions? Part of the explanation lies in the use that has been made of certain scriptural texts in thinking about this issue. One such text is 2 Corinthians 6:14-17:

Do not be mismatched with unbelievers. For what partnership is there between righteousness and lawlessness? Or what fellowship is there between light and darkness? What agreement does Christ have with Belial? Or what does a believer share with an unbeliever? What agreement has the temple of God with idols? . . .

"Therefore come out from them,
and be separate from them, says the Lord,
and touch nothing unclean."

Another goes like this: "Happy are those who do not follow the advice of the wicked, or take the path that sinners tread, or sit in the seat of scoffers" (Ps. 1:1).

Texts such as these from the Bible (and sermons preached about them) instilled in me a strong sense of separation from Hindus and the Hindu faith, and made it very difficult for me to think of praying in a Hindu temple.

Ganga, on the other hand, was influenced by Hindu scriptural texts and practices. These texts more often celebrated the *similarities* between different religions than the *differences*. Ganga often quotes two such texts. One is from the most ancient scripture of Hindus, the Rig Veda, which says, "Truth is one; sages call it by different names."

The other is a couple of lines from a famous Hindu saint who praises God (Siva) in this way:

Lord Siva of the southern land [South India], we praise you!
God of the people of all nations, we praise you!

In interpreting this text, Ganga would say that the "God of the people of all nations" is the one who is worshiped as "Siva of the southern land." Therefore, when he is in a Christian church he is worshiping the same God who is known as Siva in South India.

When I was growing up, I would not have even entered a Hindu temple. I was taught that to do so would be a betrayal of Christian faith. Once, when I visited a famous Hindu temple near Madras, I had a fever and a headache the next day. One of my friends told me that my visit to the temple was the cause of my illness, and that I should confess that sin to God so that I might be healed!

My own history has also brought about this posture of separation. When my ancestors converted to the Christian faith from Hinduism, they destroyed the Hindu shrines in our village and built Christian churches in their places. Such a dramatic conversion meant that separation from Hindus and the Hindu faith was very important to my ancestors. Understandably, it led to a severely negative attitude toward Hinduism as such. In some cases this separation meant not only that one took on a new faith, but that one took on a new geographical location as well. When large numbers of people converted to Christianity, they often moved to new locations and built "Christian" villages. I come from one such village in South India, which was named "Nazareth" by my forebears.

Yet experiences I have had over the past thirty years have led me to question the wisdom of such a posture toward people of other religions. From a protected Christian environment in small rural towns like Nazareth I moved to multireligious urban settings like Madras and Calcutta, where I had to rub shoulders with people who do not profess Christianity. The Hindus and Muslims whom I came to know as friends impressed me by their genuine piety and sincere devotion to God. They have nudged me to look for other ways of relating to them and their religions than the one I grew up with.

This experience is not peculiar to me. Increasing numbers of Christians all over the world are beginning to look at the people of other religions in ways different from our earlier attitudes. Why this change of attitude? Why do people look for fresh ways of relating to people of other religious traditions? Why do we feel uncomfortable with our earlier attitudes of separation and superiority? Is not the Christian faith the same yesterday, today, and forever? Should Christians look for a new way of living their faith in this new situation? What is it that is new about our situation?

What is new about our situation? For one thing, people of other religions no longer live far away in some exotic country; they are our neighbors in our cities and towns. They work with us in our offices, schools, and hospitals. This has been true of countries in Asia for several centuries. For example, Christians form only 2.6 percent of the total population of India, while Hindus compose 82 percent, and Muslims 12 percent. That means that in India, even those Christians who live in protected Christian environments as I once did will, at one time or another, meet and interact with adherents of non-Christian religions. There was a time when the people in my village would need to go to the neighboring Hindu village to meet Hindus, but no longer. Since the arrival of a spinning mill and a college of liberal arts in Nazareth, several Hindu families have moved in, and there is now even a Hindu temple there.

Today this is true of communities, towns, and cities in the West as well. For example, there are nearly four thousand Hindu families living in Atlanta, in addition to several thousand Muslims, Jews, Baha'is, and Buddhists. Have you ever heard someone say that there are more Muslims in the United States than Episcopalians or Presbyterians? It's true! Chances are good that at some time in your life you will have an experience like this: your family physician, who is a Hindu from India, will recommend that you see a Jewish surgeon, while your blood work is done by an African American Muslim technician and your postsurgical care is assigned to a nurse who is an American Baha'i. The proximity of all these men and women of other

11

religions among us brings an awareness that we were not capable of just a few years ago.

Every time I take groups of seminary students to visit the Hindu and Sikh temples in Atlanta my students are impressed by the generosity and hospitality of the people they find there. The Hindus welcome us gladly into their sanctuary and offer us the fruits and sweets that have been blessed by God. The Sikh worship always ends with a meal that every visitor is invited to join. But more than simply inviting us, the Sikhs insisted that we stay for the common meal! When we sat down to eat, one of my young students whispered into my ear, "We are not this friendly and welcoming in our churches, are we?" A Tibetan Buddhist monk once came to address my students. He stood in front of us in his saffron robe, speaking to us about the compassion we all need to practice. Looking at him, we were keenly aware that he was not only talking about compassion; he was himself an embodiment of compassion. My students learned that day that it is one thing to read about Buddhism and quite another to meet a practicing Buddhist! Time and again it is the same: When we come to know individuals of other religions as fellow humans, we are struck by their piety, devotion, and goodness.

Perhaps not all of us live in big cities and towns where there is a recognizable presence of people of other religions. We may live in small towns and may not come in contact with Jews, Hindus, or Muslims. But we all have easy access to the written traditions of other religions—thanks to the work of historians and Christian missionaries over the past two centuries. One can walk into almost any bookstore or library and get a copy of the Bhagavad Gita (Hindu Scripture), Koran (Muslim Scripture), or the teachings of Buddha, all translated into English. Every time I read these sacred writings, I am struck by the common themes that surface in all of them, while

I am equally gripped by the strangeness of each book. For example, the Koran opens with this prayer:

> In the name of Allah the Gracious, the Merciful.
> All praise belongs to Allah, Lord of all the worlds,
> The Gracious, the Merciful,
> Master of the Day of Judgement.
> Thee alone do we worship and Thee alone do we implore
>   for help.
> Guide us in the right path—
> The path of those on whom Thou has bestowed Thy
>   blessing,
> those who have not incurred Thy displeasure,
> and those who have not gone astray.

Once, I replaced the word "Allah" in this prayer with the word "God" (since "Allah" is simply the Arabic word for "God") and used it as an opening prayer in a Christian gathering in my town. The Christians in the audience had no idea that I was reading from the Koran. When I asked a few what they thought of the opening prayer, they all said that they found the prayer helpful. When I told them that it came from the first chapter of the Koran, they were surprised at its similarity to Christian prayers.

In the Bhagavad Gita, the Scripture of Hindus, one reads the teachings of Krishna, who is the incarnation of God. In the last chapter, Krishna says:

> Bear Me in mind, love Me and worship Me,
> Sacrifice, prostrate thyself to Me:
> So shalt thou come to Me, I promise thee
> Truly, for thou art dear to Me.
>
> Give up all things of law,
> Turn to Me, thine only refuge,
> For I will deliver thee
> From all evils; have no care.

These words sound almost like Jesus' teachings in the Gospels. Once we discover such similarities between Christianity and other religious traditions, it is very difficult for us to dismiss other religions as simply the work of the devil.

The amount of common beliefs and practices that we share with our Jewish friends is astoundingly large. Jews and Christians share the Ten Commandments, the summary of these ten in two commandments, the Psalms, and other prophetic utterances. Two-thirds of Christian Scripture is the Scripture of the Jews! Once we take this common heritage seriously, how can any Christian embrace the idea that the Jews are "from the devil"?

Access to and appreciation of the scriptures of other religious traditions forces us to feel uncomfortable with our earlier approaches to people of other religions. These men and women are no longer the same old neighbors we have had for centuries; they have become our *new* neighbors!

William Carey, one of the foremost Protestant missionaries of the nineteenth century, described the people among whom he was going to work as "poor, barbarous, naked pagans, as destitute of civilization, as they are of true religion."[1] Carey was a great missionary and rendered significant service to the people of India. Even today the people of West Bengal honor him as a champion of their culture and language. But Carey's perception of other people was tinted by the colonial attitudes of his day. When European nations were colonizing various parts of Asia and Africa, Western culture did look superior, and appeared to Europeans as the only true "civilization." It seemed that the rapid expansion of Christianity would eventually mean the demise of all other religions of the world. When the Student Volunteer Movement made "The Evangelization of the World in Our Generation" its motto, it displayed the widespread sense of optimism at the time about the expansion of Christianity throughout the world.

Today we are in a different situation. The nations of Africa and Asia have gained independence from the colonial powers and now assert the greatness of their own religions and cultures. Far from disappearing from the globe, religions other than Christianity have revitalized and are now missionary religions themselves. This point was brought home to me by a visit to Leicester, William Carey's hometown in England. When I traveled to Leicester some years back, a friend took me around to see places of interest. As we passed by a building we noticed a sign that read, "The Sanatana Hindu Temple." My friend asked me, "Do you see that, Thomas?"

I said, "Yes. There's nothing surprising about it, though, given that the majority of the residents of this city are Hindus."

"There is something more interesting here," he said. Taking me closer to the building he pointed out a stone tablet on the wall that read, "William Carey Memorial Baptist Church." The memory of Carey is now celebrated by Hindus who worship in the building that was built in his honor! I was struck by how this represents a reversal of what happened in my hometown of Nazareth in South India, and how it proves that religions other than Christianity are very much alive and flourishing in our midst. We ourselves, removed from the colonial perceptions of earlier times, can begin to value these other cultures and religions. We find ourselves affirming the worth of other religious perceptions, beliefs, practices, and lifestyles.

Once we give up colonial perceptions, we begin to recognize more and more how personal and social history, landscape and geography, and other ecological factors shape the way we think, act, and envision the world and our place in it. Though such things as history and geography do not *determine* the way we think and act, they do decisively *shape* our beliefs and perceptions. Let me give you an illustration. When we greet a person in English, we say something like, "We warmly welcome you!" Yet in my mother tongue (Tamil) we never say this. Instead, we always say, "We coldly welcome you!" or, "We welcome you with a cool heart!" Why? Because the weather in South India is consistently warm and most often hot (ninety-five degrees or above), and cool represents for us something to be desired more than warmth. Therefore our view of affection and love is shaped by the climate we live in!

This is true not of language alone; it is true of our religious beliefs as well. For example, listen to the words of "Christ, Whose Glory Fills the Skies," by Charles Wesley:

> Dark and cheerless is the morn
> Unaccompanied by Thee;
> Joyless is the day's return,
> Till Thy mercy's beams I see;
> Till they inward light impart,
> Glad my eyes, and *warm my heart*. (italics added)

Now hear how a contemporary Tamil hymn writer, Dayanandan Francis, expresses a similar idea:

> The melodies of the heart and the tongue
> are songs that speak of gratitude;
> Come and sing the songs of Zion
> for endless years with our *hearts made cool*.
> (author's trans.; italics added)

While "warm my heart" represents devotion to God for Wesley, Francis expresses his love for God with "hearts made cool"!

One can see how the story of exodus shaped the understanding of God among Jews and Christians, how the situation of warring factions within Arabia influenced the Islamic views on God and community, and how the domination of priestly Brahmins in the Indian subcontinent colored the Hindu perception of the universe. Thus we come to realize how each religion has been shaped by such things as history, geography, and climate. We recognize, more than ever before, the peculiarity and uniqueness of each religion. Each religious tradition has its own individuality because each has taken shape in particular historical and geographical circumstances. Such an understanding brings with it a sense of parity among the various religious traditions of the world. In this new situation Christian faith is invited to take its place as *one* of the religions of the world.

As commentators are fond of telling us, the world is a smaller place. No longer is it necessary to travel by air or sea to communicate and interact with those of other regions and cultures. As I am typing this chapter in my computer, I am very much aware that I can send a message through the Internet and correspond quickly with someone in another part of the world. I can pick up the telephone and call my friend Ganga in India and talk to him about this chapter. Advanced communication technology and transportation systems have brought the people of the world into closer proximity with one another. This has helped make us all aware of our interconnectedness and interdependence. The local and the global now interact in ways we could not previously have imagined. This global interconnectedness is as much a matter of politics and economics as it is of communication technology, which means that all our problems have become global problems. These global problems have to be addressed by the global community and not simply the Christian community. This means that Christians will be increasingly drawn into interaction and conversation with other religious communities in our mission to serve humanity. We are compelled to take the worldviews of other religionists more seriously than before, and this again has its impact on the way we look at people of other religious traditions.

Once we recognize that we are in a new situation, we need to search for novel ways of relating to people of other religious traditions. Are there treasures within the Bible and our tradition that can help us? What possible ways of relating can a Christian adopt? These questions have become important ones for us today. In the chapters that follow we will look at different modes of relationship between Christians and others.

Note

1. William Carey, *An Inquiry into the Obligation of Christians to Use Means for the Conversion of the Heathen* (1792; reprint, London: The Carey Kingsgate Press, 1892), 63.

CHAPTER 2

God Saw That It Was Good!

Whenever Ganga and I visit the main Hindu temple in our city, I am struck by the variety of images of God that attract one's attention in the temple. Depicted there are various forms of God, such as Siva, his consort Parvathi, Ganesh—the elephant-faced god—and various other gods and goddesses. In fact, Hindus believe that there are 330 million forms of God! In the temple there are several square-shaped courtyards, and there are images or icons in each of the courtyards. Most of the worshipers who come to the temple are not distracted by the multiplicity of images; rather, they go straight to their favorite image of God, offer their worship, chat with friends whom they may meet in the courtyards, and leave the temple.

For me, it has not been easy. Whenever I go to the temple, I find the many images of God rather distracting. First, the Christian insistence on the *oneness* and *singularity* of God makes me wonder about the polytheistic appearance of the Hindu temple. Of course, I know that Hindus do believe in the oneness of God and consider the various gods and goddesses as differing forms of *one* God. Yet I am simply perplexed and confused. Second, these images seem to pull me in all directions. My Christian upbringing trained me to focus on a single altar in the sanctuary, and the very architecture of the churches in and around my hometown was geared toward such a single-minded focus. By contrast, Ganga appears very focused and unperturbed by the somewhat "distracting" and "disturbing" plurality.

When asked how he is able to remain focused in the midst of such variety and plurality, Ganga would point out that the multiplicity of images represents, for the Hindu, an affirmation and celebration of plurality. He never tires of quoting the text from the Rig Veda that says, "Truth is one; sages call it by different names." He would also mention that the Hindu believes in multiple paths to God, called *margas*, and that each person is free to choose the path he or she wants to follow. Three such paths are the path of knowledge *(jnana marga)*, the path of devotion *(bhakti marga)*, and the path of action *(karma marga)*. Of course, Ganga would never limit the number of paths to three. For him and many Hindus, there are as many paths to God as there are different and individual human beings. He seems to revel in plurality!

These conversations with Ganga have led me to ask, What about the Christian tradition? Are there resources within the Christian tradition that enable us to affirm and celebrate plurality? Or is the Christian faith so totally controlled by "one Lord, one faith, one baptism, one God and Father of all" (Eph. 4:5-6) that Christians must shun plurality? Does the Christian faith present one and only one picture of God's love and concern for the world? Or are there multiple portraits and images of God within the tradition? These questions have driven me to the Bible; and I have discovered that the Bible, in its account of the story of God and God's mighty acts, does not fail to celebrate plurality. Therefore, I invite you to travel with me through the pages of the Bible to discover how the biblical accounts celebrate plurality and multiplicity in the universe!

GOD SAW THAT IT WAS GOOD!

Let us start at the very beginning. The Bible opens with the story of creation. In chapters 1 and 2 of the book of Genesis, there are two accounts of creation. Though these two accounts may differ in their presentation of the process of creation, one thing is quite clear in both the accounts; that is, the whole creative act of God is a celebration of the many. When the "formless void" takes form, it assumes *many* forms: sun, moon, stars, plants, trees, fishes, birds, and animals. Every act of creation is followed by the refrain, "And God saw that it was good." What a celebration of plurality! Interestingly, the command that God gives to all living creatures is to "be fruitful and multiply!" Note the word: multiply! God is not content with the number God has created; God wants many more! And God wants the creatures to engage in the creative act of fostering plurality!

This celebrative mood is reflected in the creation of humanity. "God created humankind in [God's] image, . . . male and female [God] created them" (Gen. 1:27). God builds right into the creation of humanity the celebration of plurality and difference by creating them male and female. God's loving insistence on plurality is wonderfully reflected in the account of creation in Genesis 2. While God found everything to be good, the only thing God disliked was this: "It is not good that the man should be alone" (Gen. 2:18). Isn't it wonderful to see how God prefers plurality over against singularity? Anyone who reads these creation accounts is and should be struck by God's preference for plurality.

Some may raise an objection here. Is not the affirmation of the goodness of plurality part of a portrayal of the paradise (the garden of Eden), found only in the first two chapters of Genesis? Does not the Fall take place in chapter 3, when the first couple sins? Should not we say that the multiplicity and variety we see around us are only the product of human sin? Can we continue to affirm plurality in the midst of human sin? These are very important and highly pertinent questions. But when we travel further into the story that unfolds in the pages of the book of Genesis, it is apparent that even in a world corrupted by sin and evil, God opts for plurality. Let me draw on a few stories in the book of Genesis.

First, the account of the beginnings of civilization in chapter 4 is a dramatic account of the variety and multiplicity in human civilization. Lamech, one of the descendants of Cain, has three sons, Jabal, Jubal, and Tubal-cain, and they become, according to the biblical story, the ancestors of three different strands of human civilization. Jabal becomes "the ancestor of those who live in tents and have livestock," Jubal becomes "the ancestor of all those who play the lyre and pipe," and Tubal-cain makes "all kinds of bronze and iron tools" (Gen. 4:20-22). What an affirmation of the variety of human cultures and civilizations!

Second, the well-known story of Noah and the ark is yet another example of the celebration of plurality. The story begins with God's feeling of pain and sorrow over the state of affairs in the world. "The LORD was sorry that he had made humankind on the earth, and it grieved him to his heart." God decides to "blot out from the earth the human beings . . . together with animals and creeping things and birds of the air" (Gen. 6:6-7). Yet God decides to preserve not just Noah, but Noah and his family, and a remnant of all the living creatures of the universe. God could not let go of God's love for variety! One can imagine a conversation between Noah and God:

Noah: You mean I should collect a pair each of *all* living beings?
God: Yes, Noah. I want them *all.*

Noah: Don't you want to do an intelligent selection here? This is your one chance to choose only those you like and leave out the rest! I don't much appreciate the giraffes, because I think you had lost your sense of proportion and symmetry when you created them. Do you really want the giraffes? Even if you want the giraffes, I'm sure you don't want me to take a pair of rattlesnakes and a pair of mosquitoes, do you?

God: I do, Noah. I want them all . . . all of them . . . in all their variety and difference! Please, Noah, I want them *all* to be preserved.

Is this not a stunning picture of God's desire for variety and difference? Moreover, the sons of Noah bring a colorful array of human races and civilizations into existence, as presented in the genealogy of nations in chapter 10.

Third, the story of the tower of Babel should be seen as yet another example of God's celebration of plurality and difference. This story begins, "Now the whole earth had one language and the same words" (Gen. 11:1). Hailing from India, I have always read this text as a description of heaven! In India, we have about twenty-five major languages and several hundred dialects. In such a country one wishes that one had one language, as the people of Genesis 11 did. Our attempt to make Hindi the national language has not been an easy task and continues to be a bone of contention among different linguistic groups. But in the story of Babel, God is not pleased with the one-language formula. God sees that such a one-language formula leads only to human pride and rebellion, and therefore God comes down and confuses their language. The story ends, "So the LORD scattered them abroad from there over the face of all the earth" (Gen. 11:8). Is it not crystal clear that God loves a plurality of languages, even at the expense of humans' not readily understanding one another? God could not tolerate the sound of only one language! Here again we see God's preference for plurality. As we continue reading the story of God's dealing with the people Israel, we see how God affirms and celebrates variety and difference.

When we come to the later prophets—such as Micah and Amos—the celebration of plurality is highlighted again. For example, Micah writes,

> They shall all sit under their own vines and under their
> own fig trees,
> and no one shall make them afraid;
> for the mouth of the LORD of hosts has spoken.
> For all the peoples walk,
> each in the name of its god,
> but we will walk in the name of the LORD our God
> forever and ever. (Mic. 4:4-5)

This passage is not simply about the variety of cultures, vines, and fig trees. It even speaks about the variety of understandings of God and the multiplicity of names for God among the people of the world. It sees the fearless celebration of that variety as a sign of the golden age to come.

Amos strikes a similar note:

> Are you not like the Ethiopians to me,
> O people of Israel? says the LORD.
> Did I not bring Israel up from the land of Egypt,
> and the Philistines from Caphtor and the Arameans
> from Kir? (Amos 9:7)

The God of the Bible is one who revels in the multiplicity of peoples, cultures, and religions, as we see in these passages from the Prophets.

The story of God continues as we move into the Gospel accounts of the life and ministry of Jesus of Nazareth. The teachings of Jesus clearly reflect God's appreciation of variety and difference. Jesus portrays the coming reign of God as a community that celebrates plurality. The reign of God is like a banquet that is open and inclusive. People from the north, the south, the east, and the west come and sit at table (Luke 13:29). The "righteous" elder son and the "repentant" younger son are both welcome to the feast (Luke 15:31-32). Sinners, harlots, and tax gatherers are invited, too. Jesus says, "Truly I tell you, the tax collectors and the prostitutes are going into the kingdom of God ahead of you" (Matt. 21:31). Thus the parables of the reign of God depict God as a generous host who invites and welcomes a variety of peoples to join the feast.

The same kind of celebration of plurality is exemplified in Jesus' treatment of those who do not belong to his own community of friends and relatives. While attending worship at the synagogue in his hometown of Nazareth, he expounds on a passage from Isaiah and explains how God's work of liberation includes a celebration of plurality. He identifies Naaman the Syrian and the widow of Zarephath as participants in God's liberative activity. Sadly, the people of his town are not too pleased with his idea of plurality and try to hurl him over a cliff (Luke 4:16-30). Jesus' visit to the house of Simon and his dining with Zacchaeus the tax collector are further celebrations of variety and difference. In the house of Simon, Jesus affirms plurality by accepting anointing by "a woman in the city, who was a sinner" (Luke 7:37). Similarly, when Jesus says to Zacchaeus that he "too is a son of Abraham," he presents a family of faith that celebrates plurality by including people like Zacchaeus on the family roster!

The Gospel According to John records a lengthy conversation between Jesus and a Samaritan woman at the well in the city of Sychar. One of the major questions raised in the conversation is, How does one deal with a variety of forms and places of worship? The woman says to Jesus, "Sir . . . our ancestors worshiped on this mountain, but you say that the place where people must worship is in Jerusalem." Jesus tells her that places and forms do not really matter when it comes to worship. He says to her, "Woman, . . . neither on this mountain nor in Jerusalem. . . . God is spirit, and those who worship [God] must worship in spirit and truth" (John 4:19-21, 24). Here again Jesus affirms plurality, though not explicitly and directly; by relativizing forms and places, he celebrates multiple ways of worshiping God.

The story of God continues with the descent of the Holy Spirit at Pentecost and the birth of the church, as we move out of the four Gospels. Pentecost is a dramatic and spectacular affirmation of plurality and otherness. The book of the Acts of the Apostles records this affirmation this way: "All of them were filled with the Holy Spirit and began to speak in other languages, as the Spirit gave them ability" (Acts 2:4). The first act of the Holy Spirit here is to open people to an appreciative recognition of the variety of languages and affirm them all! What God achieved through confusing and scattering in the story of Babel is achieved here through the disciples' speaking in a variety of languages and understanding one another. Here is a supreme celebration of plurality. When the people ask, "What does this mean?" Peter quotes a passage from the prophet Joel that envisions the last days as the time when sons and daughters, young and old, slaves and masters will all prophesy and celebrate variety and difference.

Such a celebration of plurality is continued as the story of the early church unfolds in the Acts of the Apostles. An Ethiopian official, a Roman centurion called Cornelius, "Simeon who was called Niger, Lucius of Cyrene, [and]

Manaen a member of the court of Herod the ruler" are all members of the band of early disciples, and they bring a colorful variety to the membership of the early church (Acts 13:1). Of course, Peter has to be convinced of such affirmation of plurality through a vision in which a large sheet containing all kinds of four-footed creatures and reptiles and birds is lowered to the ground and a voice invites Peter to kill and eat (Acts 10:9-16). Once Peter is convinced, he stands with confidence before Cornelius and his family and boldly announces, "I truly understand that God shows no partiality, but in every nation anyone who fears [God] and does what is right is acceptable to [God]" (Acts 10:34). What a powerful affirmation of variety and difference!

In describing the gifts of the Spirit, Paul gives us a glimpse of the pluralistic community the church is called to be. In his letters to the Christians in Rome and to the believers in Corinth, he emphasizes the multiplicity of gifts:

We have gifts that differ according to the grace given to us: prophecy, in proportion to faith; ministry, in ministering; the teacher, in teaching; the exhorter, in exhortation; the giver, in generosity; the leader, in diligence; the compassionate, in cheerfulness. (Rom. 12:6-8)

To each is given the manifestation of the Spirit for the common good. To one is given through the Spirit the utterance of wisdom, and to another the utterance of knowledge according to the same Spirit, to another faith by the same Spirit, to another gifts of healing by the one Spirit, to another the working of miracles, to another prophecy, to another the discernment of spirits, to another various kinds of tongues, to another the interpretation of tongues. (1 Cor. 12:7-10)

Thus for Paul, the church is a community that celebrates and affirms the plurality of gifts and ministries. Paul uses the metaphor of a body and its limbs to portray the character of such an inclusive and pluralistic community. As the story of God's dealings with the church continues, John the apostle gives us a picture of the final community that is to come—the new heaven and the new earth. In the final two chapters of the book of Revelation, we see a city that comes down from heaven. It is a city whose gates are never shut and where there is no night. An angel takes John through a city whose very architectural composition is a celebration of plurality:

> The wall is built of jasper, while the city is pure gold, clear as glass. The foundations of the wall of the city are adorned with every jewel; the first was jasper, the second sapphire, the third agate, the fourth emerald, the fifth onyx, the sixth carnelian, the seventh chrysolite, the eighth beryl, the ninth topaz, the tenth chrysoprase, the eleventh jacinth, the twelfth amethyst. And the twelve gates are twelve pearls, each of the gates is a single pearl, and the street of the city is pure gold, transparent as glass. (Rev. 21:18-21)

What an array of variety and difference! Not only the architecture, but also the treasures inside the city speak of a God who revels in plurality. John goes on to write, "The nations will walk by its light, and the kings of the earth will bring their glory into it. . . . People will bring into it the glory and honor of the nations" (Rev. 21:24, 26).

Our journey from the book of Genesis to the book of Revelation has clearly shown us a God who creates the world in all its multiplicity, variety, and difference, and revels in that plurality. Here is a God who is not satisfied with a singular expression of faith and obedience, but rather invites people of all nations to come to the feast and celebrate variety and difference. Now we know why the early church formulated its view of God in Trinitarian form. God is one in three and three in one. This statement is quite confusing and bizarre, but the point is clear. The God depicted in the pages of the Bible is a God whose affirmation and celebration of plurality cannot but lead us to affirm that God, in God's own self, is more than a simple arithmetic *one!* God is one in three and three in one! Conceiving God as Trinity is our way of affirming God's affirmation of plurality.

We have come back to where we began this chapter: the Christian tradition is one that values variety and difference. Brian Wren, a contemporary hymn writer, expresses this beautifully when he sings:

> God of many names,
> gathered into One,
> in your glory come and meet us,
> moving, endlessly becoming;
>
> God of hovering wings,
> womb and birth of time,
> joyfully we sing your praises,
> breath of life in every people;
>
> God of Jewish faith,
> exodus and law,
> in your glory come and meet us,
> joy of Miriam and Moses;
>
> God of Jesus Christ,
> rabbi of the poor,
> joyfully we sing your praises,
> crucified, alive forever.

CHAPTER 3

We Know and They Know Not

Tilaga, Ganga's wife, teaches history in a high school in Madurai. Tilaga is a devout Hindu, yet at the same time she is very open to other religious traditions. With her family she gladly participates in the festivals, celebrations, and rituals of other religions. Tilaga, Ganga, and I often celebrated the Hindu and Christian festivals together in each other's homes. Such festive occasions gave me opportunities to talk with Tilaga concerning our respective religious traditions. During one of our conversations, Tilaga told me about some of her colleagues at school who were Christians. "These are my colleagues, and I love them very much, and they love me as well," Tilaga said. "But every time we discuss religion, these Christian friends will tell me forthrightly, though in a friendly way, that I am going to hell because I am a Hindu, and that the only way I can ever hope to get to heaven would be to believe in Jesus and give up my Hindu religion. In the beginning I thought that these friends hated me because I was a Hindu. But now I know very well that these friends tell me all this not because of any ill will toward me; but rather because they consider it their duty of love to keep reminding me of my impending damnation! What do you say?"

I did not know what to say. I agreed with her that some of my peers in the Christian community did believe that all those who did not publicly acknowledge Jesus the Christ as their Savior and Lord were bound to end up in hell. I told her, as well, that not all Christians believe that people of other religions are damned simply because they are not Christians.

Here is one way of relating to people of other religions: We know and they know not. The basic idea here is this: Christianity is the *one and only* possessor of the truth about God and the *only* gateway to human fulfillment and salvation, and therefore all other religions can only be false and misleading. They do not lead people to a true knowledge of God or to a fulfilled life here and hereafter. This has been a dominant view of other religions in the long history of Christianity, especially during the period of missionary expansion in the past three centuries. In our own churches and communities of faith we do meet several who subscribe to this view of other religions. This view is often supported by quoting the following texts from the Bible:

> I am the way, and the truth, and the life. No one comes to the Father except through me. (John 14:6)

> There is salvation in no else, for there is no other name under heaven given among mortals by which we must be saved. (Acts 4:12)

Many interpret these texts to mean that only through Christianity can humans be saved and shown the way to heaven. This view has given and continues to give Christians strong motivation to go out into the world of other religions, proclaim the good news about Jesus the Christ, and gain converts to the Christian faith. If, in fact, the people of other religions are on the way to damnation, it is demanded rightly of good Christians to attempt to rescue them from such a tragedy. Great missionary giants such as William Carey, Bishop Heber, Francis Xavier, and others received their missionary calls in the setting of this belief. What does this view of people of other religions imply?

First, such a view casts the adherents of other religions in a disparaging light. Look at the first two verses of this missionary hymn written by Bishop Heber during the nineteenth century. Heber was a great missionary bishop in India and wrote such inspiring hymns as "Holy, Holy, Holy, Lord God Almighty," and "God Who Madest Earth and Heaven." He also wrote the following hymn:

> From Greenland's icy mountains,
> From India's coral strand,
> Where Africa's sunny fountains
> Roll down their golden sand;
> From many an ancient river
> From many a palmy plain,
> They call us to deliver
> Their land from error's chain.
>
> What though the spicy breezes
> Blow soft o'er Ceylon's isle;
> Though every prospect pleases,
> And only man is vile:
> In vain with lavish kindness
> The gifts of God are strewn;
> The heathen in his blindness
> Bows down to wood and stone.

If one reads through the other verses of the hymn, it is crystal clear that, for Heber, Christians are those "whose souls are lighted with wisdom from on high," whereas the people of other religions are "benighted," "vile," and caught in error and falsehood. Let me quote a hymn from another nineteenth-century writer:

Souls in heathen darkness lying,
    Where no light has broken through,
Souls that Jesus bought by dying,
    Whom his soul in travail knew—
Thousand voices
Call us, o'er the waters blue.

Hymns of this kind have gone a long way in shaping Christians' perception of people of other religions. The phrase "the waters blue" suggests that all the heathens live overseas. Most hymnbooks of today do not include these hymns. But the perception of the other has not changed greatly among Christians today. Perhaps Dante's portrayal of the prophet Muhammad in *Inferno* is still the way some Christians view people of other religions. Dante portrays Muhammad as cut in half from head to toe and split open with his heart, lungs, liver, and other inner parts of his body hanging out. What a gruesome picture of neighbors of other faiths!

Second, the vision of Christianity as the one and only way to God makes us perceive other religions as things to be abolished and supplanted. Julius Richter, who was appointed Professor of the Science of Missions at Berlin University at the beginning of this century, described the relation between Christianity and other religions in this way during his inaugural address:

Christianity is an exclusive religion. Wherever Christian missionary enterprise comes into contact with the non-Christian religions, it sets itself to oust them and to put Christianity in their place. . . . Christianity attempts to oust the non-Christian religions in the conviction that this is necessary to the salvation of their adherents.[1]

Notice the word "oust." Other religions are to be ousted and disposed off. Of course, Professor Richter is not speaking here with any malice or hatred against other religions. He himself notes, "Christianity is a religion of love," and holds it to be valuable and important that "the transition from the old to the new religion should be brought about with all possible patience and tender regard and by the way of inward conviction."[2] In this view there is nothing that can be compared between Christianity and other religions; they can only be contrasted. On one side stands the true and divinely instituted religion; on the other, the false and demonic religions.

Third, when other religions are viewed in this manner, the missionary endeavor is most often portrayed in military metaphors and thus promotes a militant attitude toward other religions. Another hymn from the missionary era portrays Christians as "armies" and "warriors," and implores them,

> Go to the conquest of all lands;
> All must be His at length.[3]

Mission is a war in which other religions are captured, conquered, and destroyed. This has literally happened several times over the past two thousand years. For example, the Crusades of the eleventh to the thirteenth centuries aimed at a military victory over Muslims and thus the conquest of Islam. Bishop Stephen Neill writes, "To the majority of Christian warriors Muslims were simply unbelievers, who had no right to existence, with whom no faith need be kept, and who might be slaughtered without ruth or pity to the glory of the Christian God."[4]

Charlemagne, the emperor of the Holy Roman Empire at the beginning of the ninth century, promoted Christian expansion in highly militaristic and political terms. Mandatory conversion to Christianity was often a condition of treaties, and those who opposed Charlemagne and his

"Christianizing" program were put to death. Two of the several rules that Charlemagne promulgated to compel people to the Christian faith were (1) Anyone who burns the body of a dead person, as is the pagan fashion, shall be put to death, and (2) Any unbaptized Saxon who attempts to hide himself among his own people and refuses to accept baptism shall be put to death. The colonial expansion of European nations during the eighteenth and nineteenth centuries reflects a similarly militant view of mission.

I am not saying that viewing other religions as false and misleading *necessarily* leads to a militant understanding of the mission of the church. But such a view has led to militant attitudes and actions, and it continues to have the potential for encouraging such an imperialistic view of the missionary task. Richter himself, after explaining Christianity as a religion of love, slips into militarist categories. He pleads for "a thorough acquaintance with" other religions because "such an acquaintance would seem as necessary for a missionary as is a knowledge of the enemy's field-force for a general."[5] Hymns such as "Onward Christian Soldiers," by Sabine Baring-Gould, have reiterated such a militaristic view of Christian mission:

> Onward, Christian soldiers,
> Marching as to war,
> With the cross of Jesus
> Going on before.
> Christ, the royal Master
> Leads against the foe;
> Forward into battle,
> See his banners go!

What I have described so far sounds like a crude caricature. Not all Christians who believe that the only way to God is through Christ have this view of other religions. There are those who are baffled by such questions as, What about those who lived before the birth of Jesus? What about those who have never heard about Jesus Christ, through no fault of their own? Is it fair to punish them with eternal damnation? What about babies who have died without knowing Christ? These and other such questions have toned down the "We know and they know not" approach in two different ways.

First, there are some who prefer to separate the question of the destiny of those who have not accepted Christ from the question of how we should perceive people of other religions. We know from the Bible that only the Christian religion offers the way of salvation through Christ. Therefore, we know that religions other than Christianity *do not* lead their adherents to the salvation offered in and through Christ. But we do not know how God will judge others. If God chooses to bring them into the fold by ways other than what we have known in the Bible, then it is God's own doing and we have no way of knowing it at all. God has chosen to reveal to us that those who do not believe in Christ are lost. But God has not revealed to us the other possibility—which is a real possibility for God! God moves in mysterious ways! Who are we to question God?

According to this view, the people of other religions definitely do not know the way of salvation, and they need to be brought into the Christian fold. Yet we need not be militant about this task, because we recognize the sovereignty and mystery of God. Therefore we will continue to announce a word of condemnation to all religions other than Christianity and invite them to turn to Christ. But we will not prejudge the destiny of all those people who reject the Christian offer.

Second, there are others who see that there is a world of difference between claiming that *Christianity* is the sole possessor of truth about God and asserting that only in *Christ* God's revelation and human salvation are available. Christianity, as a religion, is like any other religion. But Christ is unique and final. One of the leading proponents of this view was the well-known theologian of this century, Karl Barth. For Barth, religion as such symbolizes the human attempt to reach God. Of course, God is unreachable and unknown. Humans can never know God on their own. So a human attempt to reach God through religion is an attempt to "grasp at God." Such an attempt is only a manifestation of a lack of faith, and thus can only be called "unbelief." Religion is unbelief. In religion, humans "bolt" and "bar" themselves against God's revelation "by providing a substitute, by taking away in advance the very thing which has to be given by God."[6] So all religions are forms of idolatry. God can be known only in and through God's own revelation, and religions as human attempts to reach God fail to provide any knowledge of God. Where do we then find God's own revelation? That revelation has come in Jesus the Christ. Christ is the revealed Word of God, attested in Christian Scripture and proclaimed by the church. In the face of such a revelation of God in Christ, all religions are to be judged as "unbelief" and thus condemned. Barth rightly titled the chapter in *Church Dogmatics* in which he discusses these ideas, "The Revelation of God As the Abolition of Religion." All religions, including Christianity, are to be condemned and "abolished."

What I have summarized so far is only the first part of Barth's argument. According to this first part, Christians should view all religions as those to be "ousted." In the second part of his argument, Barth is able to privilege the Christian religion in a special way. When revelation abolishes religions, it is not simply a negative act. There is a positive side to this abolition. That is, "Revelation can adopt religion and mark it off as true religion." Just as there are "justified sinners," there can be a true religion, and the Christian religion can be that true religion. How is this possible? we may ask. Barth wants us to remember two things. First, when we say that the Christian religion is the true religion, we do not mean that *our* Christianity is the true religion. *Our* Christianity is our own doing, and in that respect it is unbelief like any other religion and is abolished by the revelation in Christ. Yet Christianity as God intends it to be, or Christianity as a religion of grace, is the true religion. The truth of the Christian religion rests on "the victorious grace of God." Second, as a religion that houses and announces the name Jesus Christ as the point at which God's revelation meets us, Christianity can become the true religion. It is not yet. It can become the true religion. The name of Jesus Christ is its only justification for existence. Other religions, as long as they do not carry the name of Jesus Christ, are abolished by Christ's revelation.

Two leading ideas are common among those who take the position, "We know and they know not." The first idea is that Christian faith is the true religion and all other religions are false and misleading and therefore need to be ousted and replaced. The second idea is that the truth of Christianity demands that we see *no* points of contact between Christianity and other religions with regard to the question of truth. There is a total discontinuity between Christian religion and other religions. Therefore, it is wrong to speak of similarities between Christianity and other religions. There can only be a sharp contrast.

For three primary reasons, most Christians today find it difficult to maintain the exclusive claim for Christianity that this chapter describes. First, Christians who have established relationships with people of other religions find this position to be contrary to their experience. The Muslims, Jews, and others we know have impressed us as being deeply committed to their faith and exhibit a sincere trust in God, so that we find it extremely difficult to dismiss them all as bound for hell. Quite often the commitments and lives of people of other religions challenge our own faltering Christian obedience. Both Tilaga and her husband live a life that is guided by a devoted dependence on the grace of God. In the face of such goodness, grace, and mercy, it is not easy to take an exclusive attitude and condemn them to God's eternal damnation.

Second, as we have seen, we live at a time when we are acutely aware that all religions have been shaped in the cradle of history. Particular religious ideas, distinctive rituals, and peculiar visions of the meaning of life have all been influenced by local, regional, and national histories. In such a situation, how does one claim to be the sole possessor of truth? Some may say that we know Christ or Christianity to be the only truth because the Bible tells us so. That argument holds only if we totally overlook that other religions have their own scriptures, which they consider authoritative with regard to religious beliefs. Such a multiscriptural situation makes judgments based simply on the Bible debatable. It was easy to sing as children, "Jesus loves me, this I know; for the Bible tells me so!" It is easy to argue this way about the love of Jesus when we have already taken the Bible to be authoritative for our judgments. But today both adults and children find this argument insufficient, because we are speaking about the place of other religions, and in that context the Bible is not the only scripture. People of other religions have their own scriptures.

Third, we are increasingly aware that we live in an interconnected and interdependent world in which all our problems are global ones and call for global solutions. We need to work together with people of other faiths to face the situations in our world today. "We know and they know not" does not help us in any way to engage in conversation and joint ventures. It seems to close the door even before we begin the conversation. We need to look for other ways to relate to people of other religions. To those we turn in the following chapters.

Notes

1. Julius Richter, "Missionary Apologetic: Its Problems and Its Methods," *The International Review of Missions* 2 (1913): 522.
2. Ibid., 523.
3. Hymn number 586 from *Hymns: Ancient and Modern*, as quoted in E. C. Dewick, *The Christian Attitude to Other Religions* (Cambridge: Cambridge University Press, 1953), 42.
4. Stephen Neill, *A History of Christian Missions* (New York: Penguin, 1964), 113.
5. Richter, 528.
6. Karl Barth, *Church Dogmatics*, vol. 1, pt. 2 (Edinburgh: T. & T. Clark, 1956), 303.

CHAPTER 4

We Perhaps Know; They Perhaps Know; Who Knows?

Several years ago, when my daughter was twelve years old, she raised an unexpected question during one of our conversations: "Daddy, are you religious?"

I was taken by surprise and shock. "What a strange question to ask her father. Doesn't she know that I am a minister of the Church of South India and a Christian theologian? What is going on here?" I thought to myself. So I asked her in return, "What do *you* think?"

She surprised me again by telling me, "You are not, Daddy!"

"Really? What do you mean?" I pursued.

She said, "You know what I mean. You are not a kind of fanatic, a religious fanatic!"

"Oh, thank you. That is very helpful. But I am a minister, you know, and so if I am not religious, what do you think I am then?" I asked.

She was quick to say, "You are *spiritual*, Dad! You are *not* religious!"

This conversation reveals the emerging popular use of the term "religion." Religion has had bad press! It represents, for many, dogmatism and uncritical acceptance of ideas and concepts. At its worst it is superstition, and at its best it is misplaced concreteness. This perception of religion has been formed, I think, in two different ways. First of all, we have come to be skeptical of religion on so-called scientific grounds. A kind of popular scientism dictates that what one does not see, hear, touch, smell, or taste cannot be ascertained with firmness.

In some of the Tamil Hindu traditions, three sources of knowledge are upheld. They are *kaatchi* (perception or experience), *karuthal* (inference), and *urai* (Scripture or the authoritative word of saints). All three are taken as sources for religious knowledge. For example, there are three ways to know if there is fire on top of a mountain. The way of *kaatchi* is that of seeing the fire with our own eyes and feeling the heat of it. The way of *karuthal* is to infer that there is fire on the top of the mountain because we see smoke rising up from the top. Where there is smoke, there should be fire. The way of *urai* is saying, "I know there is fire on the mountaintop because the morning headlines said so. The newspaper is an authoritative source for my knowledge about what happens on the top of the mountain." Thus religious beliefs are sustained by direct perception and experience, logical and inferential argument, and the authority of Scripture and tradition.

Popular "scientific" knowledge accepts the first two as sources of knowledge and rejects the third as totally unreliable. The existence of God cannot be ascertained either by *kaatchi* or by *karuthal*. It can be ascertained only on the authority of Scripture, which is of course highly questionable. Therefore, the popular view looks at religion with great suspicion and doubt. If we go with this kind of thinking, then the way to perceive the relation between one religion and the other will only be, "We perhaps know; they perhaps know; who knows?" We can only throw our hands up in total skepticism. The issue of which religion is the best of all becomes absurd and totally irrelevant.

Perhaps most people do not operate with the popular "scientific" view I have described here. We are living in a time when most scientists completely disassociate themselves from this almost simplistic view of matters, especially religious matters. Science itself claims knowledge that is not limited to such simple *kaatchi* and *karuthal* sources of knowledge. What are attractive to most people, however, are the anthropological and sociological studies of religions that cast serious doubt on religious beliefs. One of the most frequently quoted anthropologists of today is Clifford Geertz. In his book *Interpretation of Cultures*, Geertz defines religion as a "world-view," or "symbol-system," which humans create "to make sense of our experience, to give it form and order." Building visions about human life and its meaning is as important to humans as their biological or other needs. But humans present these visions as though the visions coincide completely with the actual state of affairs in the world. We make them appear "actual" because of our emotional needs and our need to act in the world. Geertz writes that a worldview represents a way of life and is made "emotionally acceptable by being presented as an image of an actual state of affairs of which such a way of life is an authentic expression."[1] Geertz's definition, while affirming the importance of religion in human affairs, expresses a subtle and nuanced doubt about the truth claims of religion. Look at the phrase, "being presented as an image of an actual state of affairs." The pictures of the world, life, and humanity supplied by religion need not have a one-to-one correspondence with what actually is the case. Religion claims to possess such a correspondence so that humans will have a way of committing themselves to it.

People who are influenced by this line of thinking approach religions with a deep sense of doubt and skepticism. For them, the relation of Christian faith to other religions can only be, "We perhaps know; they perhaps know; who knows?"

Some others may not have this set of philosophical or "scientific" difficulties with regard to religions. But as serious students of the various religions of the world, they are aware of all the demonic activities that have gone on throughout history precisely in the name of religion. One can narrate a long list of evils that religions have caused. Wars have been waged in the name of religion. Look at some of the areas of conflicts in today's world. In Bosnia, rivalry between Christians and Muslims has caused much of the bloodshed. In the Middle East, religious loyalties have played a major role in thwarting every attempt at peace between Israel and her neighbors. In Sri Lanka, both Buddhism and Hinduism have failed to help achieve a peaceable resolution of the Tamil-Sinhalese conflict; rather, these two religions have only fanned the flames of hatred and war. Religious differences have accentuated conflict in Ireland, as well. In Punjab, India, the Sikhs are demanding a nation of their own, named Khalistan, and religions have not been a great help in bringing peace there. We could cite many more examples of such conflicts and tragedies.

Such a reading of the religious history of humankind causes one to ask, Does any religion know truth at all? Should we not be humble enough to say, "We perhaps know; they perhaps know; who knows?"

A digression may be appropriate at this point. I have met over the past seven years several people in the West who are so overtaken by guilt over the atrocities of the Christian West in the past that they go to the extreme of saying, "We know not; they know!" Such persons exaggerate the evils of the past and the present. For example, some view the missionary enterprise of the church over the past three centuries as nothing more than colonialism, imperialism, deculturation of peoples, and oppression. They fail to recognize that while the missionary history is marred by instances of exploitation and the devaluation of other cultures and religions, scores of people in several parts of the world have found liberation and meaning through the preaching of the gospel. My own ancestors, who were Hindus, heard the good news of the gospel, preached by missionaries from England, as that which liberated them and helped them to affirm and assert their self-worth and dignity. Another example is how some women see Christian faith as incurably sexist and beyond any repair, without recognizing that in certain parts of the world, the Christian gospel has proved to be a source of liberation for women, though in limited ways.

Christians who are overburdened by the mistakes of the past also tend to romanticize other religions. They tend to say, "See how compassionate and poised the Buddhists are! See how the Hindus have a marvelous and unifying view of the universe! What an inspiration it is to watch thousands of Muslims stand together and say their prayers and do their gestures all together in such harmony!" They fail to recognize that Buddhists have not always been compassionate to others. Hindus have oppressed the people called "untouchables" in the name of a unitive view of the universe. Muslims have not always stood for harmony and togetherness. So a romantic view of the other makes some Christians say, "We know not; they know."

Let us return to our earlier line of argument. In the views we have described so far it is clear that people do not feel very confident about the Christian faith and define their relationship with people of other religions in mostly skeptical terms. In such a setting, many prefer to relate to people of other religious traditions in a nonreligious or secular way and not raise the question of each other's religious commitments at all. The Marxist criticism of religion as "the opium of the people" has significantly dampened people's hopes in religion as a whole. In all these, the approach that is highlighted is, "We perhaps know; they perhaps know; who knows?"

There are two major problems with this approach. While we note these problems and discuss them, we should bear in mind that this approach is an option, among others, for Christians. One may use the prophetic critique of religious rituals and practices within the Bible to support such an approach. For example, Isaiah writes,

> What to me is the multitude of your sacrifices?
>   says the LORD;
> I have had enough of burnt offerings of rams
>   and the fat of fed beasts;
> I do not delight in the blood of bulls,
>   or of lambs, or of goats. . . .
> bringing offerings is futile;
>   incense is an abomination to me. . . .
>   learn to do good;
> seek justice,
>   rescue the oppressed,
> defend the orphan,
>   plead for the widow. (Isa. 1:11-17)

One finds similar sentiments expressed in the writings of Micah (6:6-8) and Amos (5:21-24). The Amos passage ends with the famous verse, "Let justice roll down like waters, and righteousness like an ever-flowing stream" (v. 24). Christians who hold this view see the concern of justice and peace in the world as much more important than how one understands the place of religions in the scheme of salvation. There is truly such an emphasis within the biblical tradition and in the ministry of Jesus himself, which is highly critical of religion and places a bold question mark on all religions. We saw earlier how this biblical tradition has been used by theologians to argue precisely the opposite of what we are discussing here. For example, Karl Barth, whom we considered in chapter 3, relativizes all religions; of course, he does this only to highlight the revelatory character of the Christian faith over against religions.

Now we return to the two problems. First, the Christian tradition is confident about what it knows. The biblical story beginning with Abraham is a story of confidence in God against all odds. I find the story of the three messengers' visit to Abraham (Gen. 18:1-15) very illustrative of this confidence. Abraham receives the three visitors with these words: "Let a little water be brought, and wash your feet, and rest yourselves under the tree. Let me bring a little bread, that you may refresh yourselves, and after that you may pass on—since you have come to your servant." One can sense Abraham's confidence in the goodness of the universe. Visitors and strangers have their own role in God's work. Abraham receives the visitors with gladness. After the meal, the visitors surprise Abraham by saying that he and Sarah are going to have a son. Abraham is silent and perhaps is pondering over this all-too-sudden announcement. Sarah overhears it from the tent and laughs. Sarah's mind quickly travels through *kaatchi, karuthal,* and *urai* sources of knowledge, and it is clear to her that her having a baby at this stage in her life can only be a joke, and she laughs. But ultimately, Abraham and Sarah together live by an unimaginable confidence in the power and love of God.

One can go through the stories in the Acts of the Apostles and see how the early church expresses its confidence in the loving power of God. The healing of the man near the pool in the temple by John and Peter (chap. 3), the martyrdom of Stephen (chap. 7), the journeys of Paul, the ministry of Peter, and other events mark the church's confidence. I am aware that this confidence can degenerate into dogmatism and exclusive attitudes. But the confidence that we find in the biblical tradition is a realistic confidence—confidence in the changeless love and abundant grace of God. Paul writes, "He who has prepared us for this very thing is God, who has given us the Spirit as the guarantee. So we are always confident" (2 Cor. 5:5-6a). Christian life is not limited to saying, "We *perhaps* know."

The question before us is, How do we relate to people of other faiths, given our confidence in the fullness of life offered to us by God in Jesus Christ and through the Holy Spirit? Those who do not have confidence in the Christian faith may not see relating to people of other faiths as a problem or a question at all. It is our confidence in and commitment to the Christian faith that makes the question of our relationship with people of other religions complex and difficult.

The second problem is that the kind of skepticism that we have outlined in this chapter, though interesting at times and attractive to many, is not something one can consistently live by. Life demands from us commitments and confident action. We are faced every minute with decisions and choices. If we consistently maintain that "we perhaps know; they perhaps know; who knows?" we will not be able to act. We must make decisions and choices. We may remember Elijah's words to the people of Israel, when he invites them to quit limping with doubts and fickle-mindedness. "How long will you go limping with two different opinions? If the LORD is God, follow him; but if Baal, then follow him" (1 Kings 18:21). Even those who appear to be thoroughly skeptical have strong beliefs on some matters and are willing to suffer for those they are committed to.

The approach I have described in this chapter is one option among several others regarding how one can relate to people of other religions. As we have seen, it has its own problems. Therefore, we move to look at other options in the chapters to come.

Note

1. Clifford Geertz, *Interpretation of Cultures* (New York: Basic Books, 1977), 140, 127.

CHAPTER 5

What We Have Is Good for Us; What They Have Is Good for Them

Once, I invited a Jewish rabbi to address my students. I was teaching a course on understanding the mission of the church in today's world of diversity and difference. I had asked the rabbi to address two questions: What is the mission of the Jewish people today? and, What is the mission of Christians? The rabbi took up the first question and went to great lengths in explaining how the Jewish people saw themselves as "the light to the nations," and how this entailed both a great privilege and an awesome responsibility. Then he went on to answer the second question. The rabbi said, "I have a simple and very brief answer to the question as to what I think Christians ought to be doing. It is this: Leave us alone!" The students, all of whom were Christians, gave a chuckle of embarrassment and waited for a further word from the rabbi. The rabbi told us the story of how, as a boy, he had been beaten up by a Christian classmate who said, "Hey, my Sunday school teacher taught us that *you* killed *our* Jesus!" He further narrated how the history of Europe is stained with the blood of the Jewish people. Given such a history of hostility and conflicts between Christians and Jews, the rabbi argued, the mission of

Christians should be to leave people of other religions alone!

There are many who agree with this rabbi. We should practice what I may call a benevolent indifference that will keep us away from conflicts and confrontations. In the same way, when two children fight between themselves, some parents might ask each of them to sit in different corners of the room in order to keep them away from trouble. Quite often, you might hear the parents shout out to one child, "Why don't you leave the other alone?" If people of different religions keep to themselves and do not meddle in the affairs of others, then there will be peace and harmony among religions.

Fear of conflict is not, of course, the only reason why some recommend this approach of mutual indifference. One may recommend "benevolent indifference" for other reasons as well. The people of other religions whom we come to know in our work settings and neighborhoods are such loving and caring human beings that we find it presumptuous on our part to invite them to embrace the Christian faith. If their religious faith is helping them live with such grace and poise, who are we to recommend our religious faith to them? I have met many Hindus, Muslims, and Jews who have challenged my hesitant obedience to the call of Christ by the exuberance of their goodness and love. During my graduate studies, I came to know Robert as my neighbor in the dormitory. Rob was a member of the Baha'i religious community. He was very committed to his religious faith, and in everything he did he radiated graciousness and generosity. As a foreigner, I found Rob to be a person who helped me to adjust to living in the United States. I was always touched by his willingness to help. If I were to judge the Baha'i religion on the basis of the quality of life that I encountered in Rob, I would have to say that the Baha'i faith does a pretty good job! Therefore, I am tempted to say that if the Baha'i faith can produce a person like Rob, the best option for me is to leave him and his religion alone. Who am I to judge the religion that nurtures Rob in such love, peace, and kindness?

Many of us have stories of such encounters. The people we have known among other religious traditions do seem to lead fulfilled and flourishing lives. Even if we have not met such people, we do encounter such people when we read the biographies of the saints in other religions. When we read the autobiography of Mahatma Gandhi, *My Experiments with Truth*, we are deeply moved by his keen sense of God in his life and his sincere commitment to serving others. We also know that the Hindu faith, especially the Hindu Scripture (the Bhagavad Gita), was his greatest source of nurture and nourishment. We feel compelled to say that the Hindu faith was good for Gandhi and a host of other Hindu saints over the centuries. We may say similar things about other religious traditions as well. For example, the founding guru of the Sikh faith, Guru Nanak, was a saintly man who worked for the bringing together of Hindus and Muslims in India during the sixteenth century. Furthermore, the faith, courage, and tenacity of the Jewish people during times of persecution such as the Holocaust give us a glimpse into the spiritual depth and the moral temper of the Jewish faith. The rabbi who visited my classroom was, after all, right in asking us to leave him and his religion alone! If that is the case, should we not say that our religion is good for us and their religion is good for them? Is that not the most appropriate way of approaching people of other religions?

There are a few more reasons behind this approach to other religions. Historians of religion, sociologists, and anthropologists have helped us see that each religion is so distinctive and different from every other that the most appropriate way of respecting the integrity of other religious traditions is to leave them alone. The emphasis here is on the uniqueness and individuality of each religious tradition. Ernst Troeltsch, a German theologian and philosopher who lived in the early part of this century, grappled with the historical relativity of each religious tradition. He examined the way the Christian faith makes claims to absoluteness and universality. Troeltsch found that human history is "an immeasurable, incomparable profusion of always-new, unique, and hence individual tendencies, welling up from undiscovered depths, and coming to light in each case in unsuspected places and under different circumstances." The birth and development of each religion is full of surprises and novelty. Each religion's claim to absoluteness is shaped and influenced by the "intellectual, social, and national conditions among which it exists."[1]

This means that Christian faith has been shaped by historical, social, and intellectual conditions. So naturally for us who are Christians who live among such historical conditions, Christian faith is valid. But its validity is only *for us.* Troeltsch went on to say that the Christian religion is "final and unconditional for us, because we have nothing else, and because in what we have we can recognize the accents of the divine voice."[2] But this does not exclude the possibility that people who are in historical and cultural settings different from ours may experience God and God's grace in an entirely different way through a different religion. Religions are so dissimilar in their origin, development, and context that it would be unwise to make judgments between them. We would do well to leave them alone. Troeltsch did not use the phrase "leave them alone," but he made a similar appeal with the following two statements: First, "We cannot live without a religion, yet the only religion that we can endure is Christianity, because Christianity has grown up with us and has become a part of our very being." Second, "There can be no conversion or transformation of one into the other, but only a measure of agreement and mutual understanding."[3] In other words, let us agree to disagree, and let us be civil about it.

There are those who view the invitation to religious conversion as an infringement on the integrity and freedom of a person and his or her religion. For example, Mahatma Gandhi was vehemently against the idea of religious conversion on the basis that one should be left to follow the religion of his or her own country, family, and community. During the days of the struggle for political independence in India, Gandhi developed the idea of *swadeshi,* which means "of one's own country." He engaged the concept mainly to oppose the dumping of British goods and services on the people of India, and invited Indians to stand on their own feet, employ their own resources, and cherish their own traditions. His calls to boycott clothes made in England, to make salt from the waters of the Indian Ocean, and so on were based on the idea of *swadeshi.* Gandhi extended the idea to religions, too. The people of India have their own religion, namely, Hinduism, and they do not need any other. Of course, this does not mean that other religions are to be opposed and chased away from the soil of India; rather, the "leave one another alone" formula was foremost in the mind of Gandhi. He firmly believed that all religions were equally true and hence religious tolerance is to be practiced by leaving people of other religions alone.

What I have described so far as "benevolent indifference" is becoming a predominant approach to people of other religions among Christians today. Christians who are burdened by the guilt of our past, in which we persecuted, subjugated, and attempted to annihilate other religious traditions and the people who followed them, find the idea of mutual indifference very attractive. Since most of the religions are more or less good, true, and beautiful, let us leave each religion to find its own ways of making its adherents better people. Let Christians be better Christians, Hindus better Hindus, and Muslims better Muslims, and so on. There are two other factors in our contemporary life, as well, that make this approach acceptable to many.

The first factor is the recent emergence of "the postmodern view." Though the postmodern view takes several varied forms, one may say that there is one overarching theme running through the various postmodern theories and philosophies. At the risk of oversimplification, let me state the idea this way: There is no one grand story within which one can fit all the differing stories of humans. There is no metanarrative. What does this mean? In the past, we have seen the movement of human affairs in patterns that give us a way of deriving a meaning, an aim, and a direction to human history. Some of us saw the story of humanity as a story of God's action in the world. Therefore, by looking carefully at the story of God, we were able to discover how the various religions are interrelated and how they all come together in a tapestry of humanity's colorful movements toward the divine. Various metaphors were used to describe that tapestry, such as all rivers leading to the same ocean, a ray of light bursting forth to a rich rainbow of colors, and so on. For some others, the story of God reiterates Christianity's status as the true religion, because the revelation of God is only to be found in the Christian faith.

Those who find the idea of God difficult to accept find in *history* as such the coming together of all various religions and movements of humanity. History, for some, is that grand narrative within which we can locate the little histories and stories and recognize an interconnected web. This view, while recognizing the differences among individual religious traditions, sees them all within "the universal law of history" as the individual and novel manifestations of the one grand movement of history. Postmodern thinking questions both these grand narratives—God's story and history—and exposes them as particular, biased, and oppressive pictures of human history proposed by the powerful in each society. History is exposed as "his" story—the story of men in power and control. If such is the interrelation between religions and religious traditions, then the best approach is to leave one another alone. There is no way in which one can compare or contrast religions; each is unique, peculiar, and different. Each religion is a local story—and let it be so!

The second factor that makes "benevolent indifference" appealing is that we are beginning to recognize how the traditional bonds among individuals within the setting of family, community, and nation are breaking down, giving rise to extreme forms of individualism. Let me give you a mundane illustration. There is a custom in the part of India I come from regarding the celebration of young children's birthdays. The child will take a tray full of candy and visit his or her friends' and relatives' homes. Friends and relatives will pick up a piece of candy and ask the child, "What's the matter?" The child will say, "It is my birthday!" Then the friends and relatives will wish the child a happy birthday, and in most cases, give the child a gift in return. In 1980 and 1981 I was in the United States, away from my family. On my daughter's birthday, I took a tray of candy and went to my friends in the dormitory. The first four people to whom I offered the candy gave me a lovely smile and said, "No, thank you," and walked away. The only thought they had in mind was, "Do *I* want to eat a piece of candy?" Because none of them wanted to eat any candy, they simply said no and moved on. I was so frustrated that when I approached the fifth person I said, "Please pick up a piece of candy and ask me 'What's the matter?' " She asked me, and I was able to tell her that it was my daughter's birthday! This illustrates that the question, "What do *I* want?" is primary in our society. If we apply this to our religious situation, it is clear that if we live by the dominant individualism of our day, we should simply allow people to choose and live by the religion they want. What he or she chooses is good for him or her; and what I choose for myself is good for me. Live and let live!

For all its appeal to a postmodern society, this approach has a few problems as well. For one thing, our religious traditions have not *always* been good for us; nor have they been good for *all* of us. When some African Americans in the United States choose to become Muslims, they are illustrating how the Christian religion has *not* been good for them. Christianity is seen as racist, oppressive, and unable to meet the spiritual demands of African Americans. Similarly, the Hindu faith has not been good to those Indians who have been considered "untouchables" and placed at the lowest rung of the social ladder. The Indian caste system has been nurtured by the Hindu faith, and therefore the outcasts of Hindu society see the Hindu faith as their enemy and decide to move to other religious traditions. During the grand era of the Christian missionary movement of the past three centuries most of those who embraced the Christian faith in India came from the so-called untouchable caste. A group of them converted to Buddhism in large numbers during this century as well. Such religious conversions gave occasions for the oppressed groups to gain their dignity and assert their self-esteem. There are many women who find Christianity both inherently sexist and extremely oppressive, and they are not willing to say, "What we have is good for us." They are looking for other ways of expressing their religiosity. Such examples can be seen in every religious tradition. Our religious traditions have not always been good for us.

I know an acclaimed Christian preacher in India who, though born and brought up in a staunch Hindu home, became a Christian during his time in a Christian college in India. His conversion to Christianity is an apt illustration of what I am talking about here. As a young college student, he was bombarded by a lot of questions regarding his own spirituality. He would often go to his teacher, who was a Hindu and a professor of philosophy at the college, with his questions. This went on for several months. One day, the Hindu professor told the young man that his quest might be helped more by what Christ symbolizes, and asked him to read the Bible and talk to a few Christian leaders. The young man did what his teacher recommended, was soon attracted to the figure of Christ, and became a Christian. What a marvelous story! A Hindu professor tells one of his Hindu students to explore the Christian faith! He could have said, "Hey! You are a Hindu, and it is good for you!" Instead, he pointed him to Christianity. As far as this young man was concerned, the Hindu faith was not adequate for him in his spiritual quest.

Similar moves have been made by Christians in the West who have been dissatisfied with the Christian faith and have moved to embrace the Hindu faith. I heard about a Hindu monk in Atlanta, Georgia, who had established a spiritual center and was conducting meetings and meditations regularly. My friends recommended that I invite him to speak to the students in my class. So I telephoned and talked to the monk, and we decided to meet in my office to plan our session. On that day Swami (as he is often called) came to my office door and knocked. I opened the door, expecting to meet an Indian Hindu monk in saffron clothes. Instead, there was in front of me a white American dressed in slacks and a shirt who greeted me with a smile of compassion and grace! We sat down to talk. I learned how Swami, a child of Christian missionary parents, found the Christian faith to be inadequate for his spiritual quest and became a monk of the Ramakrishna Mission of the Hindu faith.

These two stories illustrate very well how people should be free to choose, switch, quit, and change their religious affiliations. It is, in a sense, an infringement on the freedom of people if we say that the religion that people inherit is good for them.

A second, much more serious problem with this approach is that it is not as simple as it appears. We live today in such an interconnected and interdependent world that "good for us" and "good for them" are not two separate categories. If all the Hindus lived in India, all the Muslims in one of the countries in the Arabian peninsula, all the Sikhs in Punjab, all the Buddhists in Sri Lanka, and all the Jews in Israel, we may be able to talk about "good for us" and "good for them" separately. Even in such situations, our economic, commercial, and political ties are such that we must face the question of what is good for *all* of us! But our world today is not in such clear-cut religious compartments. As I noted in the first chapter, people of other religious traditions live in proximity to us in our families, neighborhoods, cities, and nations. Therefore, "live and let live" and "leave one another alone" just do not match up to the plurality we find among us. We cannot afford to exist on our own. We need to interact with one another, help one another toward a common vision of what is good for us all, and share our resources to face the local and global challenges of today.

WHAT WE HAVE IS GOOD FOR US

Notes

1. Ernst Troeltsch, "Christianity Among World Religions," in *Christian Thought: Its History and Application* (Westport, Conn.: Hyperion Press, 1935), 22-23.
2. Ibid., 26.
3. Ibid., 25, 30.

CHAPTER 6

We Know in Full; They Know in Part

The apostle Paul had just arrived in the city of Athens. He was waiting for his friends Silas and Timothy to join him soon. In the meantime, Paul started exploring the city of Athens. There were temples everywhere dedicated to a variety of Greek gods and goddesses. "He was deeply distressed to see that the city was full of idols" (Acts 17:16). But this distress was only one part of his experience of Athens. He had also met some Epicurean and Stoic philosophers, and they were always ready to debate with him. They showed a keen interest in what he had to say about Jesus the Christ. Paul could remember the writings of some of their poets and philosophers, as well. This mutual interest in one another's religious beliefs and practices led to a session in which Paul could present what he had to say. On that day Paul stood in front of them and spoke to them about his belief in the crucified and risen Lord, Jesus Christ.

Paul's speech at Athens represents another way of approaching the people of other religious traditions. His approach had three elements. First of all, Paul recognized and affirmed the religiosity of the Greeks. He said, "I see how extremely religious you are in every way" (Acts 17:22). He appreciated their piety. He even quoted from their writings to substantiate what he had to say about

Jesus the Christ. He acknowledged that the religion they followed was not all false and misleading. Second, Paul went on to point out how their religion signaled a quest for something more than what they already had in their tradition. He interpreted the inscription on an altar, "To an unknown God," to mean that the religiosity of these people was leading them to quest or long for something that they yet needed to know. In a way, the Athenians publicly acknowledged through the altar for the unknown god that their knowledge of God was partial and that they were awaiting fuller knowledge and revelation. Paul was appreciative of that quest as well. Third, Paul proceeded to present Jesus the Christ as the full and complete revelation of God that the Athenians were anticipating. Christ was "the unknown god" they had always wanted to know. God, according to Paul, did not condemn the religion of the Athenians. God overlooked their "times of ignorance" or partial knowledge and invited them to a fuller life through Christ.

With this, Paul presents another approach to the people of other religions: "We know in full; they know in part." One need not and should not say that the religions other than Christianity are totally false and misleading; rather one should note that they are partial and inadequate. They belong to the infancy of human history, and "when the fullness of time had come, God sent [Christ] . . . to redeem" all through faith in Christ (Gal. 4:4, 5). Other religions are not devoid of any knowledge of God; rather, they are preparations for the coming of Christ. Paul had the same kind of approach to other religions when he was in the town of Lystra and preached to the people there. He said, "In past generations God allowed all nations to follow their own ways; yet [God] has not left [Godself] without a witness in doing good" (Acts 14:16-17a). So we know in full; they know in part. In other words, what other religions offer is partial, preparatory, and poised toward the perfect. What Christian faith offers is full, complete, and perfect, because Christ is the fullest manifestation of God's love, care, and offer of salvation. What Paul wrote in his passage on love is true here, too. He wrote, "When I was a child, I spoke like a child, I thought like a child, I reasoned like a child; when I became an adult, I put an end to childish ways" (1 Cor. 13:11). The relation between the Christian faith and other religions is somewhat like this. Other religions represent the speech, thought, and reasoning of a child; Christian faith is an adult faith, fully developed and mature. This is so not because individual Christians are perfect. No, not at all. It is the revelation in Christ that is full, perfect, and final.

This is the stance which Christianity had taken toward the Jewish faith right from the days of the early church. The New Testament writers are quite convinced about the preparatory character of the faith of the people of Israel. The Jewish Scriptures are interpreted time and again as pointing to the coming of Christ in Jesus. For example, the writers of the four Gospels, Matthew, Mark, Luke, and John, often quote the Jewish Scriptures to make the point that what had been foretold by the prophets and eagerly awaited by the people of Israel had been fulfilled in Christ Jesus. In reporting the birth of Jesus, Matthew uses three different passages from the Jewish Scriptures. Jesus' birth in the little town of Bethlehem had been, according to Matthew, foretold by the prophet Micah (Mic. 5:2); the miracle of virgin birth by the prophet Isaiah (Isa. 7:4); and the massacre of children by King Herod by the prophet Jeremiah (Jer. 31:15). This method of viewing the Christ as fulfilling the longings and expectations of the Jewish people is carried right through the Gospel of Matthew. Mark opens his Gospel with prophecy from Isaiah, and Luke presents Christ as the fulfillment and climactic point of the history of humanity by giving us the genealogy of Jesus. There are several places in the Gospels that appeal to texts from the Jewish Scriptures and view Jesus as the fulfillment of the expectations of the Jewish people. We do not need to look at each of them.

Not only do the Gospel writers present Christ as bringing a fullness to what was partial and incomplete, they also show us a Jesus who in himself is aware of such fulfillment. In the Sermon on the Mount, Jesus explicitly states, "Do not think that I have come to abolish the law or the prophets; I have come not to abolish but to fulfill" (Matt. 5:17). Then Jesus goes on to elaborate on how this fulfillment happens with regard to some injunctions in the Law of Moses, such as rules concerning murder, adultery, swearing, and love of neighbors. Each of these teachings is presented so as to imply that Jesus perfects the law that was previously partial and incomplete. In Luke's Gospel, Jesus claims the prophecy in Isaiah regarding the servant of God for himself and announces, "Today this scripture has been fulfilled in your hearing" (Luke 4:21). Thus the Jewish religion is seen as a preparation for the coming of Christ Jesus. So one can say that we relate to people of other faiths with the notion that we know in full and they know in part.

One of the classic texts that echoes this approach is found in the Epistle to the Hebrews. We may well hear the preface to the Epistle.

> Long ago God spoke to our ancestors in many and various ways by the prophets, but in these last days [God] has spoken to us by a Son, whom [God] appointed heir of all things, through whom [God] also created the worlds. He is the reflection of God's glory and the exact imprint of God's very being, and he sustains all things by his powerful word.
>
> (Heb. 1:1-3)

If we take this seriously into account, each of us can view the religion of our ancestors as that which God used in previous times to speak to us; but God has now spoken to us through Christ, who is the *"exact imprint of God's very being."* One can interpret this to mean that every revelation before Christ is not the "exact imprint," though there is definitely a partial and approximate revelation of God. In Christ, though, the fullness of Godhead has met us.

The history of Christianity over the centuries bears witness to this approach as well. Let me give you two examples, one from the early church fathers, and the other from the modern missionary movement of the past three centuries. The church fathers saw Greek philosophy as God's way of preparing humanity to receive the good news in Christ Jesus. For example, Clement of Alexandria wrote, "Philosophy tutored the Greeks for Christ as the Law did the Hebrews." This is quite clearly seen in the way in which the early Christians, starting with John, were willing to employ Platonic, and Neoplatonic ideas in their exposition of Christ and the salvation he brings.

During the modern missionary movement, as well, several missionaries recognized the good in the traditions of the religions of Asia and Africa and often viewed them as God's way of preparing the people to accept the gospel of Christ. I have mentioned earlier how my hometown Nazareth came into existence as a "Christian" village due to the work of the missionaries nearly two hundred years ago. I am sure the missionaries had only a bare minimum of local vocabulary and a heavy load of European accent to communicate. It is always a wonder to me that such preaching of the missionaries in the local language made sense to my people and they decided to become Christians. Such amazement nudges one to say that the people had already such a sufficient (though not full) amount of knowledge of God that they were able to recognize the good news of the Christian gospel and commit themselves to it.

Some of the missionaries were quite articulate about this approach. One such missionary was J. N. Farquhar. He was the Literary Secretary of the National Council of YMCAs in India and Ceylon in the beginning of this century. He published a book entitled *The Crown of Hinduism*, in which he ably argued that each aspect of Hindu life and thought was aware of its inadequacy and was looking forward to a fulfillment, which only Christian faith can meet through the figure of Christ Jesus. After examining several Hindu ideas, beliefs, and practices, Farquhar says that "Christ provides the fulfilment of each of the highest aspirations and aims of Hinduism." He closes his voluminous book with the following statement:

> Every line of light which is visible in the grossest parts of the religion reappears in Him [Christ] set in healthy institutions and spiritual worship. Every true motive which in Hinduism has found expression in unclean, debasing, or unworthy practices finds in Him fullest exercise in work for the downtrodden, the ignorant, the sick, and the sinful. In Him is focused every ray of light that shines in Hinduism. He is the Crown of the faith of India.[1]

I may sum up what I have said so far in this way: Other religions and people of other faiths are not necessarily on the way to damnation. They are in a posture of journeying toward God and God's love. Yet their religions offer them only a partial and imperfect glimpse into what God has to offer to us all. This knowledge prepares the people of other religions to hear, understand, and accept the good news in Christ Jesus. While we appreciate the rays of light we discover in other religions, we should approach them as pointers to Christ and not as possessors of the full revelation in Christ. In other words, at best other religions can offer to their adherents only the questions—important and valuable questions. They only set their adherents on a quest; but it is Christ who offers the answer to their questions and the fulfillment of their quest.

This approach is attractive to many Christians, for several reasons. First of all, there is an appreciative understanding of other religions in this approach. Those religions are not all false and misleading; rather, they are oriented toward God, though inadequately and imperfectly. Such a view enables one to view a person of another religion as a fellow traveler on the path toward the divine. Second, one can defend this approach with much biblical support. Notice how Paul, Matthew, Luke, and Mark seem to operate with this approach. Third, the missionary task of the church appears more as a gentle and persuasive invitation to fuller life than as a militant ousting of other religions.

While we recognize the attractiveness of this approach, we should not fail to acknowledge some of the problems in this approach as well. Let me bring my Hindu friend, Ganga, into the discussion here. How do I find his spirituality? What do I think of his relationship with God? I have known Ganga for years and therefore I can describe his spirituality with confidence. I must confess that I do not see Ganga as simply being on a quest. He boldly bears witness to me that he has found God's love in the religious tradition that has nurtured him from his childhood. He, at times, would even remind me that it is more accurate to say that God has found him rather than that he has found God! Interestingly, both Ganga and I have had long discussions on the concept of grace in our respective traditions, and he has always surprised me with his deeper understanding and authentic experiences of God's grace. In the face of such encounters with a person of another

71

religion, I cannot envision him as anything other than a fellow pilgrim who is as much a child of God as I am.

Just as the spiritual depth of the lives of our friends from other religions challenges the "We know in full; they know in part" approach, a careful study of other religious traditions will tell us that other religions are not simply quests. They are both questions *and* answers. The Hindu saint Manickavacagar has written many hymns and poems in praise of God. In one of the hymns, he cries out that he is weary of being born again and again on this earth. This is in accordance with the Hindu belief that one goes through a cycle of births and deaths. His cry has always reminded me of what Paul had to say in his Epistle to the Romans: "Wretched man that I am! Who will rescue me from this body of death?" (Rom. 7:24). The most fascinating thing here is that *neither* Paul nor Manickavacagar stops with the cry of weariness; both of them assert the freedom they have experienced in their encounter with God. Paul writes, "Thanks be to God through Jesus Christ our Lord!" (Rom. 7:25), and Manickavacagar praises Siva (God) for coming down as a guru to meet him, enlighten him, and liberate him. So other religions are not simply sets of questions; they do not merely represent a quest. They also offer ways of salvation. We may not agree with those ways, and we may not choose those as our ways of attaining fuller meaning and life; but to reduce other religions to quests is to distort them and fail to respect their integrity. It is a violation of the ninth commandment, namely, "You shall not bear false witness against your neighbor." Let my neighbor tell me what his or her religion means to him or her. Let me not reduce it to a mere quest.

This is true of the Jewish faith as well. Although the New Testament writers have often interpreted the Jewish Scriptures as a preparation for the gospel of Christ Jesus, we want to be more discerning and more sensitive in our interpretation. We are sadly aware that our reduction of the faith of the Jewish people to a mere endless quest has resulted in our blatant persecution and intolerance of our Jewish brothers and sisters. The Jewish Scriptures do not simply ask questions; they offer answers as well. For example, when the prophet Micah stacks up a set of questions like,

> With what shall I come before the LORD,
> and bow myself before God on high? . . .
> Will the LORD be pleased with thousands of rams,
> with ten thousands of rivers of oil? (Mic. 6:6*a*, 7*a*)

He also gives us the answer in such succinct words as these:

> [God] has told you, O mortal, what is good;
> and what does the LORD require of you
> but to do justice, and to love kindness,
> and to walk humbly with your God? (Mic. 6:8)

Therefore, to define the faith of the Jewish people as an endless quest would be an expression of disrespect to the wholeness and integrity of the Jewish tradition.

There is another serious flaw in the "We know in full; they know in part" approach. Even if we are able to argue for this approach in relation to religions that existed before the birth of Christ Jesus, how do we take account of those religions that came into being after the advent of Christ? For example, Islam emerged, as a religion, during the seventh century C.E. Moreover, Islam understands itself as the final revelation of God after the coming of Jesus, the Christ. Muslims recognize Jesus as one of the prophets and would see Muhammad as the decisive and final messenger from God, and Koran as the fullest revelation of God, while the Jewish and Christian Scriptures are preparations for the coming of Muhammad. To think of Islam as a preparation for the gospel of Christ almost borders on the absurd, does it not?

Consider the religion of the Sikhs. Sikhism is a religion that emerged in sixteenth-century Punjab, India. It began as a way to fulfill the quest of both Hindus and Muslims in one religion, namely, Sikhism. The first guru of Sikh faith, when he emerged from an experience of enlightenment, uttered, "There is no Hindu; there is no Muslim: all are children of God!" It would be quite reasonable to present Sikhism as the fulfillment of the quest underlying both Hinduism and Islam. More recently, the Baha'i faith, built on the revelatory experiences of Baha'i-ullah, claims itself to be the most recent and significantly fuller revelation of God for our times. Baha'is recognize Jesus and Muhammad as God's own prophets; though they would not see either of them as the final revelation of God. Furthermore, Baha'is do not claim finality to Baha'i-ullah either. They are open to more revelations from God in the future, in God's own time.

If we respect the integrity of these religious traditions, it may be difficult for some of us to relate to them with the kind of approach we have outlined in this chapter. We may have to look for other ways of relating to people of other religions, knowing that there are several Christians who find this approach to be a valid, biblically sound, and helpful one.

Note

1. J. N. Farquhar, *The Crown of Hinduism* (London: Oxford University Press, 1913), 458.

CHAPTER 7

We Know and Know That We Know; They Know and Know Not That They Know

anga and I have had long conversations on religious themes. Every time we have one, I am struck by the common features in our religions. For example, whenever he and I discuss the concept of divine grace, I am amazed by the similarities between Hindu and Christian piety. The love for God, the longing for God, the praise and adoration of God are all areas where we both come very close to each other in our religious traditions. When one experiences such affinity and similarity, one is compelled to look for ways to explain this phenomenon. One way to go about explaining this affinity is to see Ganga's beliefs as a preparation for his accepting the final word that has come to us in Christ. It is not easy for me to think of Ganga in those terms, as I have mentioned in the preceding chapter. He lives a fulfilling religious life, and I would be very reluctant to consider him purely as a seeker who has yet to find the truth. I have to look for other ways of relating to him.

Of course, we are both aware that each of our religious traditions has its own distinctiveness. But the goodness in each tradition is what brings wonderment to me. I am often reminded of the text in James: "Every generous act of giving, with every perfect gift, is from above, coming down from the Father of lights, with whom there is no variation or shadow due to change" (James 1:17). Based on this text, I may say that Ganga's religious heritage comes from God as well. In other words, "every perfect gift" within Hinduism I may say is from God. If we extend this to other religions, we may say that the light that shines in each religion is from the one God "with whom there is no variation or shadow."

Even so, as a Christian, when I talk about God I do not talk about God in general. It is always in reference to Christ and the Holy Spirit as well. Christ is the organizing center of my vision and understanding of God. God manifested God's love, grace, and mercy in the face of Jesus Christ. My picture of God is out of focus without the portrait of Jesus Christ. Therefore, it is not sufficient to say that all good gifts come from God. There should be a way to talk about Ganga's religious heritage within my portrait of Christ. If Christ is one who defines God to me, then the knowledge of God and the experience of God's grace that I find in Ganga's life cannot be understood apart from Christ. This line of thinking has led many to consider John's portrayal of Jesus Christ as "Word become flesh." John begins his Gospel with these words: "In the beginning was the Word, and the Word was with God, and the Word was God" (John 1:1). It is clear that for John "Christ" is earlier than the birth of Jesus in Bethlehem. Christ was present in the beginning of the world as "Word" or *Logos* (the Greek word for "word"). The Logos who was with God and through whom all were created is the one who became human in Jesus of Nazareth.

In adoring the Logos, John says that Logos is "the true light, which enlightens everyone" (John 1:9). Note the word "everyone." Can we not say that it is the Logos or

Christ who enlightens *everyone*, including a Hindu like Ganga? It sounds appropriate in light of John's description of the activity of the Logos. If I find rays of light, flashes of revelation, and similarity in perceptions, I should not be surprised; rather, I should recognize those as the work of Christ in the hearts and minds of Hindu believers through the ages. One may look at people of other religions, too, in this manner. The Muslims, Jews, Jains, and others who live their life in the light of God's abundant grace are actually enlightened and enabled by the Logos whom we call Jesus Christ.

The early church fathers have often spoken about what they called *logos spermatikos*. What they meant was that in every human being the Logos was present in a seed form. Therefore no one is outside the activity of the Logos. Right through the centuries, if we recognize truth, beauty, and goodness in the lives of the saints of various other religions, and in the beliefs and practices of those religions, it is all through the presence of the Logos in everyone in the form of a seed. It is that seed that sprouts and blossoms as various religious beliefs and practices. What a grand vision of the universal presence and activity of Logos!

Although this sounds extremely attractive, I find myself troubled by one question. Does Ganga call this Christ? Though I can see how Ganga is inspired by Christ the Logos in his spiritual journey, he does not call it either "Logos" or "Christ." He often refers to *arulsakti* (the power of grace that is often portrayed as the goddess Parvati, the wife of Siva) as that which enlightens him. At other times, he may refer to a text in the Hindu Scriptures which talks about the power of grace taking the form of a religious teacher and enlightening everyone. This is quite different from the first eighteen verses of the first chapter of John's Gospel, is it not? Why does he not call this reality of grace "Christ"? Can one say that he does not know that it is Christ through whom he is enlightened? Can we speak of an "unknown Christ" in Ganga's life?

Raymundo Panikkar, one of the leading Roman Catholic theologians of this century, has experienced firsthand the kind of interreligious relations we have been discussing in his own family. His father was a Hindu and his mother was a Roman Catholic. As a Christian, Panikkar combines both these religious traditions and has to deal within himself with the question of the relationship between Christian faith and other religious traditions. In his book *The Unknown Christ of Hinduism*, Panikkar asks us to consider two things before we examine our relationship with other religions and its adherents. First, he invites us to see that what we mean by "Christ" is much bigger and broader than the man Jesus of Nazareth. Using the description of Christ as Logos in John's Gospel, Panikkar helps us to see that Christ, whom we come to know only through Christ's incarnation in Jesus, is much greater than Jesus. We should recognize and acknowledge the cosmic dimension of Logos (Christ). Second, if we say that Christ is cosmic or universal, what do we mean by the word "Christ"? Panikkar offers a meaning of Christ, based primarily on the prologue to John's Gospel. Shall we say that Christ is that meeting point where the divine and the human encounter each other and enjoy bliss? Is that not what had "become flesh" in Jesus of Nazareth? Do we not see in Jesus—his life, teachings, and death and resurrection—the coming together of the divine and human in beauty and grace? Here is Panikkar's definition:

> This, then, is Christ: that reality from whom everything has come, in whom everything subsists, to whom everything that suffers the wear and tear of time shall return. He is the embodiment of Divine Grace who leads every Man to God; there is no other way but through him.[1]

Panikkar has examined the highest forms of Hinduism only to discover that what we mean by Christ is already present in Hinduism. That point at which the divine and the human meet does appear in the teachings and practice of Hinduism, especially when Hindus talk about the human soul *(atman)* being united with the Cosmic Soul *(Brahman)*. He writes, "Christianity and Hinduism meet each other in a reality which partakes of both Divine and the Human, i.e. in what Christians cannot but call Christ."[2] Of course the Hindus do not call it Christ and they do not have to. But one can boldly say that Christ is present there, as an "Unknown Christ."

Karl Rahner, another Roman Catholic theologian, comes at this issue from a different context in Europe—a post-Christian setting. Three things are clear and fundamental for Rahner. One, God has been decisively revealed in Jesus Christ once and for all; so the coming together of the divine and human in Jesus the Christ is superior and normative. Two, God as unconditional love cannot but be concerned about the salvation of all humans. The goal of the God whom we meet in the Scriptures is to save all humans. God has a universal purpose of salvation. Three, all humans are endowed with an orientation toward what Rahner calls Mystery. We can see how humans transcend their biological, physical, social, and historical environments and are on the move toward the Mystery. But this basic posture of human beings is to be combined with God's universal offer of salvation. When we combine the last two of Rahner's ideas, it is clear that all humans are living in a universe that is graced by God's offer of salvation and the human orientation toward it. It is the coming together of these two that we call the Christian experience.

Can we say that those who are not Christians do not have this experience of responding to the self-offer of God?

No, we cannot; because humans, by God's own will and pleasure, have been created with an orientation toward the Mystery. At the same time, we know that God's offer has been given to us in a unique and unrepeatable way in Jesus the Christ. Then what have we to say about those outside the Christian fold who respond to God's offer of salvation? At this point, Rahner offers what has become a well-known and equally controversial phrase. Rahner refers to those in other religions who have responded to the gracious offer of God as "anonymous Christians." They are Christians, though they are not known by that name or have not taken that name for themselves.

Both Panikkar and Rahner offer us a vision in which we can see other religions and those who follow other religions as "not far from the kingdom." Though people of other religions have not identified themselves as Christian by acknowledging the decisive revelation in Jesus Christ, they are Christians without the name Christian. This enables us to have a very positive response to other religions and people of other religions. Other religions are not religions that need to be ousted and replaced. Nor are they simply questions to which only Christianity can offer answers. They are human responses to God's free and universal offer of salvation. Of course, they need to be invited to an acknowledgment of the unique and decisive act of God in Jesus Christ. Christ is not a foreign particle that we introduce into the body of their religion. Christ is already present there, and needs only to be unveiled and made known. Since Jesus Christ is the universal savior, we still need to invite people of other religions to accept the supremacy of Christ. But such a task is done in a mode of unveiling the Christ who is already there in those religions.

During one of my conversations with Ganga, I attempted this approach. I told him, "Ganga, you may not call yourself a Christian; you may not be a Christian according to the records of the church; but you are an 'anonymous Christian.' " This was not new to Ganga, because he has read the writings of both Panikkar and Rahner. So he smiled at me, which signaled to me both approval and amazement. Then he told me, "Well, it is definitely better than being called heathen, pagan, non-Christian, or unbeliever. I do not mind being called a Christian at all. Did not Gandhi often say that he was simultaneously a Hindu, a Christian, and a Muslim? I do consider it a privilege to be called a Christian. But it is the term 'anonymous' that I do not much appreciate."

When I asked him why he did not appreciate the word "anonymous," Ganga told me that he had two difficulties with the word. First, whenever he went to the Methodist church in Cambridge, Massachusetts, he thought of himself as a Christian and participated fully in the Sunday morning worship there, including the Eucharist. He was happy that no one in that church treated him like a "second-class Christian" or an "anonymous Christian," and he fully appreciated that. Though he would consider it a great compliment to be called a Christian, he did not see the term "anonymous Christian" as a compliment at all. Second, Ganga wanted me to consider the fact that he and other believers in India have been given names by others from early days. The name "Hindu" itself is a name that the Portuguese and the Muslims gave to the religious people of India. "Now again, someone else is telling us who we are," he said. "We are now anonymous Christians! Why can we Hindus not be left to have our own distinctive name? Is not naming a kind of control? Are you not judging me and my religion purely from the standpoint of your religious beliefs?" Ganga said all this in the most gentle way one can, and with a gracious smile on his face.

I agreed with Ganga that his objections to being called an "anonymous Christian" were quite understandable and assured him that I fully respected his feelings. I did, however, tell him that the term "anonymous Christian" is put forward more as a help for Christians to respectfully appreciate the people of other religions and *not* for their going around naming and calling every other person an "anonymous Christian."

Ganga appeared pleased with my explanation. Then he went on to say, "Do you know that you are an anonymous Hindu?"

"Really? How so?" I asked.

Ganga told me, "Hinduism is not a religion; it is a way of life. In Sanskrit it is called *dharma*, which can be translated as justice, order, righteousness, and religion. *Dharma* is not fixed as a rigid order for all. Each of us has to discover his or her own *dharma* and live by it. So if you are one who is following your *dharma*, the divine order and righteousness, through your own form of Christian faith, then you are an anonymous Hindu. I would even go as far as to say that you are a Hindu, not just an anonymous one, even if you disclaim it!"

I did not look very pleased with the gracious offer of Ganga. My ancestors rejected the Hindu faith and became Christians. For them and for me, it has meant something precious. Therefore, to be called an anonymous Hindu did not sound like a compliment at all! I have also been in interreligious meetings in India where Muslims have at times made similar claims. Muslim friends have told me that the word "Islam" meant "submission or surrender," and therefore anyone who submits to God truly and fully is a Muslim whether or not he or she is a member of the Muslim community. Ganga understood my predicament and said, "I think this way of calling one another 'anonymous' does not help. It robs each of us of our particularity.

Perhaps we need to find another way of relating to one another." I agreed with Ganga.

I find this approach to people of other faiths both attractive and problematic. When I am operating within my Christian community, I find the phrase "anonymous Christian" very helpful in developing an appreciative understanding of persons of other faiths. It seems appropriate to call some of the saints of other religions "anonymous Christians" when I am preaching to a Christian congregation. People hear that phrase as "Christians at heart," and those saints no doubt were Christlike in their life and work. But once I move out of my Christian community and place myself in a multireligious group or setting, this phrase becomes extremely problematic. I feel as if I am trying to tell my neighbors in their faith who they are, and literally robbing them of their own particularity and their religion of its integrity. Perhaps we should explore more and look for other ways of relating to people of other religions.

Notes

1. Raimundo Panikkar, *The Unknown Christ of Hinduism*, rev. ed. (Maryknoll, N.Y.: Orbis Books, 1981), 49.
2. Ibid.

C H A P T E R   8

We and They Together Need to Know More!

anga and I have been active in two interreligious dialogue groups that meet occasionally for dialogue, discussion, and prayer. One group, called, Religious Friends' Circle, consists of nearly thirty persons—Hindus, Muslims, and Christians from differing walks of life. Our experiences in that group have been extremely rich and varied. There have been days when we have felt at the end of the meeting that our spirits have been enlivened, our visions expanded, and our souls nourished. At some other times, we have left the dialogue frustrated, hopeless, and discouraged because the path to mutual appreciation and learning looked distant and dim.

I remember vividly one of our meetings when a Christian in the group had made some remarks that were highly offensive to the Hindus. When one of the Hindus retorted, he compounded the problem by his own reference to a certain element in Islam, to which the Muslims took strong and loud objection. The dialogue soon turned into pandemonium, and I, as the moderator for that particular meeting, had to call for adjourning the meeting right away. I dismissed the meeting and told the people that we would see if and when we could meet again. When people began to leave the room, two marvelous things happened. First, one of the older Muslim gentlemen in the group said to me, "Sir, don't you think that we should close our meeting with prayer?" I felt ashamed, called the people back into the room, and we had three prayers—Hindu, Christian, and Muslim. Second, after we said the prayers, the group decided to meet again the next month, and they have been meeting for years to this day. Ganga and I have been part of this group for several years and have enjoyed the process of mutual learning in the group.

We were members of another small group of university professors—five Christians and five Hindus—who met every now and then in one another's homes for discussion, dialogue, and prayer. We were all, to some extent, well-read in both the Christian and Hindu traditions. Our discussions were focused, sometimes erudite and at other times simple friendly chats. One of the most moving and inspiring meetings we had was on a Good Friday several years ago. We decided to talk with one another on the theme of human suffering. The session was literally a meditation on suffering at the foot of the Cross! What a wealth of sharing and learning we experienced that day! We explained to one another, criticized one another, and learned from one another. We really experienced the text from Ephesians coming alive right in front of our eyes: "Reconcile both groups to God in one body through the cross, thus putting to death that hostility through it" (Eph. 2:16). When we had met for the first time several months earlier, Suri, one of the Hindu members in the group had said, "I hope that we will become such good friends that we will *not* criticize one another." I said almost instantly, "I am hoping that we will become such good friends that we *will* criticize one another." Suri had his doubts about my idea of friendship. But here we were on a Good Friday at the foot of the Cross as one body—supporting, criticizing, and learning from one another!

WE AND THEY TOGETHER NEED TO KNOW MORE!

What I have described here gives us a glimpse into another way of relating to the people of other religions. We may call this approach, "We and they together need to know more!" I invite you to travel with me as I attempt to unpack this approach. When we say, "We and they," we are beginning our approach with distinctions. We and they are each, individually and as groups, distinctive people. Religions are not all the same. People of differing religious traditions do, in a significant way, differ from one another. To rush into saying that we are all the same is not fair to any one of us nor to any one of our religions.

Historical, sociological, and anthropological studies have shown us that religious communities are distinct and different from one another. Each religious community has its own peculiar features, beliefs, and practices. These cannot easily be grouped into classes of religions as we have attempted to do at times. For example, some have used classifications such as natural versus revealed, this-worldly versus otherworldly, monotheistic versus polytheistic, and so on. When we look carefully at each religion, we find that religions do not easily fit into such classifications. Each religion seems to have its own particular ways of understanding God, God's revelation, and human salvation, so that it is perhaps misleading to think of a certain religious idea as the common ground.

Furthermore, we cannot even say that all religions are about God. Not all religions teach about a personal God as we Christians normally perceive God. Some Hindus believe in a suprapersonal God in the form of *Brahman*, and some Buddhists do not believe in either a personal or a suprapersonal God. Each religious tradition is distinctive. This distinctiveness is much more clear when we meet as individuals belonging to differing religious traditions. Ganga and I may discover many similarities; but we know that we are very different at the same time in our religious traditions and in the way we appropriate our own religious traditions. I am not just a generic Christian; nor is Ganga a generic Hindu. We are each particular and distinctive.

Such a picture of plurality should not alarm us as Christians. If you recall the way we portrayed the biblical affirmation and celebration of variety and difference in chapter 2, you will recognize that we should be happy to recognize these differences and celebrate diversity. The God whom we encounter in the midst of all this variety is a God who revels in the beauty of plurality. Therefore, the word "and" between "we" and "they" is an important word; we should never allow the "we" and the "they" to collapse into a third, unrecognizable mass. Such an emphasis on "and" draws us away from a third religion that combines the best in each of us and somehow becomes universal. Such attempts to form a synthetic religion for all have always failed, and even if one succeeded, it would not satisfy people in any religious tradition. We humans have our own distinctive ways of organizing our lives in this world, and hence our religions need to be and are distinctive and different.

We are *different* from one another; but we are not *distant* from one another. That is why "we and they" should be combined with "together." We find ourselves *together* in this world today. We have repeatedly mentioned how we live in an interconnected and interdependent world. I am actually typing this sentence during my visit to Bangalore, India, and this morning's newspaper, *The Times of India*, clearly depicts a world that is interconnected and interdependent. The page on international news mentions $350 million in World Bank aid to India, Michael Jackson the rock star, a Christian Dior fashion show, peace negotiations between Israel and Palestine, the issue of giving the most powerful handguns to police, and so on. All these articles indicate how our stories and histories are interlocked. The listing of cable TV programs contains among others *Teenage Mutant Ninja Turtles, The Urban Peasant, Oprah Winfrey,* and *Dynasty.* The TV channels include MTV and the Discovery channel. We live in such an interconnected world today. We should never lose sight of this fact when we think about relating to people of other faiths. All our problems are global problems, and they demand global solutions. Such global solutions have to be worked out by the people of the whole world in consultation and cooperation with one another.

Am I suggesting that we and they are together because of expediency alone? No, not at all. There are other reasons we may say that we are together. Some have maintained that we are together because there is only one God, and all religions in their varied understandings of God stand together before this one God. One can build a grand vision of all standing in awe and wonder before the one God, who has no second. Whether we call it God, *Brahman,* Allah, Ultimate Reality, or Life, we are all together. Yet Christians who are in relations with Buddhists do not always find this view of our togetherness very helpful, because many Buddhists do not believe in a Supreme Being called God.

Some others may see this togetherness in terms of our common humanity. Just our being human should bring us together. Of course, we all have our own views and perspectives on what it means to be human in this world. But our being human brings us together, one may say. Some may refine this further and say that it is our being "historical" that has given rise to this plurality, and therefore the historicity of the human is what brings us all together. There are some who claim that irrespective of our distinctive and divergent religious views and beliefs we are all, in some form or another, concerned about the well-being of this earth and all its inhabitants. I am listing these various ways in which one may understand our togetherness mainly to stress that though we are distinct from one another we are not distant from one another. We are interconnected, and we are together. Therefore, our approach to other religions should value our togetherness and take the form of "we and they together."

We and they together *need to know more!* One form of togetherness is passive and reactive, but what I am suggesting here is a togetherness that is active and proactive. If we understand ourselves relating to people of other religions in an active and proactive manner, we must feel the need for the other. One can and some do live among others with what I call a "benevolent indifference" or with a sense of self-sufficiency. We are beginning to see that this is no longer a fruitful way of relating to others. We all need to know more because our knowledge of the truth is only partial, at best. Truth is more than what we understand it to be or know it to be. A classic metaphor has been used to describe this situation. We are, each in our own religious traditions, like the five blind men who touched different parts of an elephant and described the elephant accordingly. One touched the tail and said that the elephant looked like a giant brush. Another felt the leg and thought that the elephant looked like a pillar, and so on. They were all right in what they said, but only partially. Religions are like this in their knowledge of the truth. All religious beliefs and views are only approximations of the truth. The only problem in this metaphor is that it implies there is one person who has seen the whole elephant, and that person is able to make the judgment that every vision is partial. Who could that person be? Unfortunately, none of us who belong to different religions are in a position to have a look at the whole elephant and make that judgment. Nevertheless, the idea that our concepts, ideas, and views are only approximations of the truth is well taken. If that is the case, we do need the other for our knowing more and for progressing toward the whole truth.

It is also quite apparent when we examine the history of each religion that religions have been more creative and constructive in the company of other religions than in a hegemonic situation. We have not done well either in conflicts or in separation and isolation. In our interaction with others with a sense of need, we grow and blossom as individuals and as religions. It is often the "outsider" who gives new life to a religion. My own understanding of and growth in the Christian faith have been facilitated by contact with people of other religions. The story of my continuing friendship with Ganga and his family illustrates my point. Even the awareness of one's own distinctiveness comes through such encounters. For example, Christian theology has blossomed through encounter with Greek philosophy. The word "theology" itself was born out of that encounter. We need the other. We and they together need to know more.

The ecological and environmental crisis in which we find ourselves is illustrative of this need. One religion, alone with its own ideas and spiritual resources, cannot meet the challenges of this crisis. We are increasingly aware that we need the resources of other religious traditions to help us. Together we can face the challenge much better than we can alone. Christian faith, which for centuries has emphasized the freedom of humans to dominate and subjugate nature, is discovering that we need correctives from other religions such as Native American religions, Hinduism, and others to face the environmental crisis. These are only a few examples of our need to know more together with others. One can look at the social, economic, and political problems of today and see that we need the resources of one another to act together for a better world.

The approach I have outlined so far is generally called "dialogue" or "conversation." But one may at this point ask several questions. Does not conversation happen in the approaches that we have examined in the preceding chapters? Do not people who claim Christianity to be the only true religion, people who see other religions as preparations for the coming of Christ, and people who consider people of other religions "anonymous Christians" engage in conversation? Yes, they can and they do. But the conversation that I want to describe here is sustained by certain basic affirmations about ourselves and others. It involves a strong recognition of our distinctiveness, our togetherness, and our need to pool our resources. These affirmations are important for us if we are to understand what kind of conversation we are dealing with here.

Let us look at the words "conversation" and "dialogue." Both these words are about people talking with one another. "To one another" is a more important element in this phrase than "talking." A silent dialogue may occur when two friends are sitting by the beach and watching the sun set on the ocean. When we do things together we are often engaging in active dialogue. The important element is mutuality. Therefore, we are not limiting dialogue to verbal conversation between two or more people. Every act, word, and thought carried out together with others in a spirit of mutuality can be viewed as dialogue.

I find the words of Stanley J. Samartha, one of the leading ecumenical theologians who has been engaged in the ministry of interreligious dialogue both in the World Council of Churches and in India, very helpful. Let me quote from his writings.

The basis of inter-religious dialogue is the *commitment* of all partners to their respective faiths and their *openness* to the insights of others. The integrity of particular religions must be recognized.

The objective of dialogue is not a superficial consensus. It should not lead to the dilution of all convictions for the sake of false harmony. It must lead to the enrichment of all in the discovery of new dimensions of Truth.

Dialogue should not be limited to mere academic discussions. . . . Living together in dialogue should help communities—particularly in multi-religious societies—to shed their fear and distrust of each other and to build up mutual trust and confidence.

Genuine dialogue demands humility and love.[1]

Samartha's guidelines make it clear that dialogue is not simply patting one another on the shoulder and feeling good. It is a serious matter of mutual challenge, mutual encouragement, and mutual learning. If our dialogues do not lead to mutual learning and mutual enrichment, we may simply call them parallel monologues! If our participation in dialogue does not motivate us to or spring into unified action for justice and peace in the world, our dialogues end up as nothing more than an empty babble! Samartha goes on to tell us that interreligious dialogues happen around common human concerns and "should promote deliberation and *action* on such common concerns."[2]

When we take the approach of "We and they together need to know more," we are approaching other religions and people of other religions as our dialogue partners in the journey toward a just, peaceful, integrated world. Some Christians immediately wave a red flag when they read a sentence like the one above. Have we given up our responsibility to witness to the love of God in Christ? Do we no longer invite people "to accept Christ as their personal Lord and Savior"? We have not shirked our responsibility. Rather, we have in dialogue another way of witnessing to the love of God in Christ. Our listening to others and our willingness to be corrected, changed, and nurtured by the other is one way, perhaps the most relevant way, of being in mission today. We need to remember Jesus' words to those disciples whom he sent out two by two to preach about the reign of God. Jesus asks his disciples to be ready to receive the hospitality of those to whom they have been sent and announce peace to them (Luke 10:7). Dialogue is a way of expressing Christian hospitality and graciously accepting the hospitality of others. One can see this clearly manifested in the ministry of Paul during his missionary journeys described in Acts. Dialogue is a genuine expression of humility and love.

The dialogues that Ganga and I have participated in over the years have helped us to test out our "humility and love." During one of our conversations, we discussed the place of women in Hinduism and Christianity. Ganga kept telling me that the Hindu faith believes in the equality of women and men, and therefore the subordination of women to men is a peculiarly "Christian" problem. Hindus' adoration of both the male and female forms of God is often used to support this argument. I kept quoting a few passages from the Hindu Scripture to point out that there is a vision of men as superior to women. I was trying to point out to him that the subordination of women was a problem that was not distinctive to Christian religion, but Hinduism, too, had supported patriarchy and promoted the oppression and exploitation of women. Ganga would not agree. Two weeks later, Ganga met me and told me, "Perhaps I should look at that passage you pointed out the other day all over again. You may be right!" There are other times when I have said to him, "You may be right!" Dialogue is an exercise in humility and love.

Notes

1. Stanley J. Samartha, *Between Two Cultures: Ecumenical Ministry in a Pluralist World* (Geneva, N.Y.: WCC Publications, 1996), 81-82.
2. Ibid.

C H A P T E R 9

Gentleness and Reverence

Sundar and Sita each made a lasting impression on me during a Hindu conference I attended along with Ganga. After I had presented my paper on the concept of guru (teacher) within a particular Hindu tradition, Sundar met me and wanted to have a private conversation with me. Sundar is a devout Hindu and comes from a family of dedicated Hindus. He had graduated recently from college and was gainfully employed. When we met for dialogue, he began the conversation by expressing his amazement that I, a Christian minister, had studied the Hindu faith sufficiently to have been able to present a paper on it during the conference. I thanked him for his kind words and continued the conversation. He said to me, "I want you to know that two of my brothers have renounced the Hindu faith and have become Christians by accepting baptism in the local church. My parents are not very happy with that; yet it has not completely ruined our family relationships."

I thought, "Should I say that I am very happy that his brothers have become Christians? Why not? As a minister of the church, am I not happy when people turn to Christ and become members of the church?" Expressing my joy at this point seemed a bit premature, so I probed him to tell me more.

He said, "I am not at all upset that my brothers have become Christians. What really annoys me is that these two keep telling me day after day that if I do not accept Christ and publicly acknowledge Christ by taking baptism, I will end up in hell. You are a Christian minister who has studied Hinduism. What do you say?"

I pleaded ignorance about who goes to heaven and who goes to hell, and continued the conversation by asking him about his view of his own religion and finally about Christ. "What do you think of Christ?" I asked.

He said immediately, "I admire Christ; I love to follow his teachings, too. But I do not see why I should accept baptism and become a member of the Christian church."

I replied, "That sounds really very interesting to me! Why don't you follow Christ and continue being a Hindu?"

Sundar was a bit perplexed. "Do you really think it is possible to be a Hindu and a follower of Christ at the same time?" he asked.

I continued, "How would I know? I am a Christian. You should try it out and tell me whether it is possible to be a Hindu and a disciple of Christ at the same time."

That sounded like a challenging project to Sundar. He became more and more excited and interested in continuing the conversation. We had dialogues several times during the conference, and at the end of the conference he drove me to the airport so that we could use even the driving time to continue the dialogue. At one point in the conversation he asked, "Now tell me: Why are *you* a Christian?" I told him what Christ and the Christian faith have meant to me. He wanted to know more. He asked, "As someone who has studied Hinduism, what do you think is special about Christianity for you?"

I had to do a lot of hard thinking and deep soul-searching to be able to continue my dialogues with Sundar. The dialogues with him were highly enriching in my own spiritual journey.

Sita was much younger than Sundar. She was a young woman in her late teens and appeared agitated when she told me that she wanted to speak to me. I agreed, and we met in a tent near the conference hall. Sita told me, "Sir, since you read a paper on the concept of guru in our tradition, I want to tell you something that has happened to me. I have been to several gurus and they have all disappointed me. Their words and their deeds do not match, and I am sick and tired of going to them. But don't you think that one needs a spiritual teacher (guru) to attain liberation?"

There was a voice within me telling me, "Thomas, this is a once-in-a-lifetime occasion to bear witness to Christ. Here she is, let down by the Hindu gurus. This is the right time to tell her about Christ." There was another voice within me as well, which told me, "Why be in such a hurry? Listen to her more, listen to the Spirit, and let her hear the good news of God's love through your patient and empathetic listening." So I continued the conversation, listened to her more, and asked her, "Do you really think that one needs a guru to go to God? I have learned that God accepts all of us, just as we are. We do not need any special teachers to take us to God. We can go to God directly."

She was surprised, "Really? How is that possible? Don't you know that you need a guru to teach you a *mantra* (sacred formula) so that you can repeat the mantra and find salvation?"

"I am not sure we need one. I only know that we all have equal access to God." I said. She insisted that one needed a mantra to get to God. So I asked her, "Do you know any mantra?"

"Yes, I do. It is *namasivaya.*" *Namasivaya* means "May Siva's name be praised!"

I said to her, "Why don't you recite *namasivaya?* Won't it draw you to God's loving presence?"

She was not certain whether that could be done without the help of a guru. We conversed for a bit longer, and then suddenly she looked at me with a tingle in her eyes and asked, "Who is your guru, by the way?"

I said, "Do you know that I am a Christian?"

"Yes I do. I want to know who your guru is," she replied.

I told her that Jesus Christ was my guru.

She looked pleased. "What mantra has he taught you?" she asked.

I was totally taken by surprise. My mind almost went blank. Soon I collected my thoughts and said, "Well, some Christians do use what we call the Lord's Prayer as a mantra. But as far as I am concerned, Christ has taught me that I need neither a guru nor a mantra to get to God. God is always ready to receive me into God's loving arms!"

Sita's face lit up. She got up, thanked me, and disappeared into the crowd of people in the conference. I did not see her afterwards.

Though both Sundar and Sita made a lasting impression on me, they also confused me and left me with a lot of questions. Did I do the right thing in not proclaiming the Lordship of Christ in a straightforward and simple manner? I could say that I gave both of them in some sense the gospel, the good news that God loves them dearly. But I did not give them a focused invitation to become a Christian. Did I sacrifice the proclamation of the gospel for the sake of empathetic listening? These questions have haunted me for a long time. This is so mainly because my desire to announce the good news of Jesus Christ was based primarily on certain biblical texts such as John 14:6 and Acts 4:12:

I am the way, and the truth, and the life. No one comes to the Father except through me. (John 14:6)

There is salvation in no one else, for there is no other name under heaven given among mortals by which we must be saved. (Acts 4:12)

Instead of allowing these texts to haunt me, I decided to let my experience with Sundar and Sita guide my understanding and interpretation of these texts. Before we go into a discussion of these texts, I want to say a few words about the nature and character of the Bible and the arduous task of interpreting biblical texts.

First, picking up a few verses from different parts of the Bible and basing our judgments on just those verses can be very misleading. This process is often referred to as the proof-text method. We choose the texts we like or those we think are central in the Bible and base all our beliefs and values on them. If we simply take the two verses quoted above and ask what I should have done during my conversations with Sundar and Sita, it is very clear. I should have straightforwardly announced to each of them that Christ is the only way, the only one through whom one can reach God or secure salvation. But at the same, if one looks at texts such as the following, one gets a different idea:

Then Peter began to speak to them: "I truly understand that God shows no partiality, but in every nation anyone who fears [God] and does what is right is acceptable to [God]." (Acts 10:34-35)

John answered, "Master, we saw someone casting out demons in your name, and we tried to stop him, because he does not follow with us." But Jesus said to him, "Do not stop him; for whoever is not against you is for you." (Luke 9:49-50)

Not everyone needs to be following with us. Whoever is not against us is for us! At the same time, if I use these texts to argue that we do not need to share the story of Christ and the salvation available in him, that will be equally a proof-text method, and equally problematic.

This means that we need to know clearly what kind of document the Bible is. I have found it helpful to say that the Bible is not a book; it is a library. It is a library consisting of sixty-six books. So to ask what the Bible says about our relation to people of other religions in a general way will be the wrong question. No one goes to a library and asks, "What does this library say about other religions?" It would be seen as an absurd question. Different authors may say different things on this matter. Some may not say anything at all about this. This is true of the Bible, too. We cannot simply ask, "What does the Bible say about our relationship with people of other religions?" We need to look at each author, each book, and each subsection to see what we have there.

Of course, there is a unity to the Bible in the sense that it is a collection of books with the express purpose of aiding us in our understanding of Jesus Christ and of the vision of God, humanity, and the world in the light of Christ. But at the same time, we should not forget that the Bible is a library. With these initial remarks, I invite you to closely look at the two verses I quoted earlier, especially John 14:6.

One may say, "Is not that verse quite clear? Jesus says that he is the way, the truth, and the life. To make it clearer, he adds that no one comes to the Father except through him. What is there to be explained or interpreted? The idea is crystal clear, is it not?" Perhaps it is. But those of us who have met people like Sundar and Sita begin to wonder, are not satisfied with the traditional interpretation, and want to have a fresh look at these texts. When we attempt to do so, we may come up with four possible interpretations of John 14:6.

1. Some say that since John's Gospel is more a sermon on Jesus than a verbatim account of what Jesus actually said, one may conclude that Jesus did not actually say that he was the way, the truth, and the life. It is the author, John, who puts those words in the mouth of Jesus. The Jesus whom we meet in the first three Gospels is very reluctant to claim any title for himself. When the rich young man asks him, "Good Teacher, what must I do to inherit eternal life?" Jesus replies, "Why do you call me good? No one is good but God alone" (Mark 10:17-18). Some people question whether such a Jesus would go around telling people, "I am the way," "I am the good shepherd," "I am the life," and so on. They would suggest that Jesus did not claim himself to be the way, the truth, and the life.

This interpretation, whether it is right or wrong, is not helpful to me, because whether Jesus said those words or not, John said them, and that matters a great deal to me. Do we not base our beliefs about Jesus, his life, his ministry, and his teachings on the witness of the early apostles? Is not this the reason we call ourselves the *apostolic* church? If so, John's claim that Jesus is the way and the truth and the life matters a lot to us and we should take his words seriously. He is one of the original witnesses to the events surrounding Jesus of Nazareth. Therefore, understanding these words as John's words instead of Jesus' is not a big help.

2. Another interpretation asks the question, What is the situation in which these words were spoken by Jesus? Was Jesus answering the question as to how the disciples

should relate to people of other religions? Do we hear the disciples asking that question anywhere in John's Gospel? No, we do not. Of course, the Gospel was written for Jews and Greeks who were demanding from the early Christians a clear picture of the emerging Christian identity. Who are these people who claim Jesus as Lord? What is it that makes them different from the Jews and the Greeks? These were the questions that were in the forefront in the writing of John's Gospel.

Therefore, when Jesus claims that he is the way, the truth, and the life, we see an emerging definition of what it means to be a Christian. A follower of Christ is one who takes Jesus to be his or her way, truth, and life, and one who opts for no other. Such a singular devotion to Christ is what makes people distinctively Christian. To place John 14:6 in today's multireligious setting to judge the destiny of people of other religions would be to take it totally out of its context and derive conclusions that are not intended in that verse. Even today, for Christians, Christ is the only way, the truth, and the life. God's ways—very often, mysterious ways—of dealing with other people cannot and should not be limited to this text alone.

3. There are some who invite us to understand John 14:6 in the light of John 1:1-18. John begins his Gospel with a poem on *Logos* (Word) precisely because he wants us to view and understand Jesus' life, ministry, death, and resurrection in the light of the portrait of Jesus as the Logos made flesh. This means that the one who is claiming to be the way, the truth, and the life is not simply a man called Jesus in first-century Palestine. It is the Word made flesh who is making this claim. The Logos is in the beginning with God and is God. This Logos is the light of the world, who enlightens every human being (John 1:9).

If that is how John wants us to view Jesus, we may see John 14:6 as telling us that no one comes to God except through the Logos, who enlightens everyone. Therefore, in a multireligious context, John 14:6 simply means that God is accessible to all through God's own reaching out to humanity through the Logos, and we Christians have come to recognize the Logos through Jesus who is the enfleshing of God's Logos.

4. There is another interpretation as well. We all know that the chapter divisions in John's Gospel are not John's own. John wrote the Gospel as one long and flowing piece. The chapter divisions were added much later. Therefore, we need to ask where the incident that leads to Jesus' proclamation that he is the way, the truth, and the life begins. It is very clear that the talk about "the way" begins when Peter asks, "Lord, where are you going?" Let us look at the verses that follow: "Jesus answered, 'Where I am going, you cannot follow me now; but you will follow afterward.' Peter said to him, 'Lord, why can I not follow you now? I will lay down my life for you' " (John 13:36-37). It is very interesting to see how Peter senses quickly what the journey and the way are all about. By saying, "I will lay down my life for you," he has indicated that the way Jesus is talking about is the way of willing self-sacrifice and suffering. Therefore, when Jesus tells his disciples, "I am the way, and the truth, and the life," he is actually referring to this way of self-sacrifice and suffering.

There is no other way to God, there is no other truth, and there is nothing more life-giving than self-sacrifice and suffering for the sake of others. Did Jesus not go on to say, "No one has greater love than this, to lay down one's life for one's friends" (John 15:13)? Did he not also say, "Those who love their life lose it, and those who hate their life in this world will keep it for eternal life. Whoever serves me must follow me" (John 12:25-26*a*)? Do we not hear echoes of this in the first three Gospels when Jesus says, "Whoever does not take up the cross and follow me is not worthy of me" (Matt. 10:38; cf. Mark 8:34, Luke 9:23)? Jesus in this passage is not telling us about Christians' relations to people of other religions; rather, he is pointing to the centrality of love and self-sacrifice as the only way to the heart of God, because God's heart is a wounded heart, wounded for the sake of the world.

What I have offered here are some of the possible ways of reinterpreting the text that seems to haunt all those who in their lively contacts with people of other religions want to relate to them in ways other than condemnation and confrontation. One may do a similar exercise with Acts 4:12. There again a universal claim is made by Peter in the setting of the healing of the man near the temple gate, and it would be wrong to pluck it from that context and interpret it as a text to determine Christians' relationships with people of other religions. Moreover, the word translated as "save" and "salvation" also means "heal" and "healing." That means that Peter's statement relates precisely to the healing and the name used in the process of healing. We would violate the integrity of the passage if we were to place it within today's multireligious setting and draw conclusions.

As I reflected more on my conversations with Sundar and Sita, I was gripped one day by what Peter had to say in 1 Peter 3:15-16a: "In your hearts sanctify Christ as Lord. Always be ready to make your defense to anyone who demands from you an accounting for the hope that is in you; yet do it with gentleness and reverence." This text has been a great source of inspiration to me in recent years. We are called to sanctify Christ as Lord in our lives ("heart" signifies not just one part of my personality but my whole life). We are also called to be ready at all times to give an accounting of the hope we have in Christ to those who ask it of us. They will ask it of us only when we are in a relationship of dialogue and mutuality. Even as we give an account of our hope in Christ, we need to remember that we witness to our *hope*, and not to what we have already received or accomplished in Christ. We bear witness to the hope of the reign of God and the coming together of all in God. In all this, we are asked to exercise "gentleness and reverence." Sundar and Sita demanded "an accounting for the hope that is in" me. I trust that I was gentle and respectful.

It is becoming increasingly clear to me that we need to fine tune our hearts in order to gently and reverently recognize the Spirit of God in Christ at work in the world and among the people of other religions.

Study Guide

This book may be used as a material for study in a Sunday school class, or a regular discussion or study group in your church. You may plan nine meetings with the use of a chapter at a time, each time you meet. Following are some of the questions that may be helpful in facilitating discussion. These questions are preceded by a brief summary of each chapter.

Chapter 1: My New Neighbor

We recognize that we live today in a world that has brought us into lively contact with people who profess religions other than Christianity. Such an awareness lures us to look for newer ways of understanding our relationship with people of other religions.

1. What interaction with people of other religions have you had recently? Are such contacts more frequent for you than they were ten or twenty years ago?

2. Recall occasions when the topic of how people of non-Christian religions stand before God has come up in your church or Sunday school class. How do the Christians you know typically answer this question?

Chapter 2: God Saw That It Was Good

The Bible presents us a God who creates, sustains, and celebrates variety and difference. God is not satisfied with singular expressions of piety, but invites all to revel in plurality.

1. Are there stories, events, and teachings within the Bible other than what is mentioned in this chapter that celebrate variety and difference? Share some of them with the group.

2. How have you experienced celebration of plurality in your church? Are there events, festivals, and celebrations that honor variety and difference?

Chapter 3: We Know and They Know Not

One way to relate to people of other religions is to view them as those who are in error, and who therefore should be invited to renounce their religious tradition and accept the Christian faith.

1. Do you think that this particular approach to people of other religions is absolutely essential for Christian engagement in mission and evangelism? why or why not?

2. Are there instances of your encounter with people of other religions that nudge you to question the wisdom and usefulness of this approach? Give some examples.

Chapter 4: We Perhaps Know; They Perhaps Know; Who Knows?

Religions have a history which is tainted by their failure to consistently promote human well-being and harmony. Therefore some Christians opt to be skeptical about the role of religions in human society, and choose to relate to others purely in secular terms.

1. In what ways might Christians combine in their lives a bold confidence in the Christian faith and a healthy skepticism about it?

2. Are there instances when your encounter with a person of another religious tradition has actually strengthened your confidence in the Christian faith? Talk with the group about one of those times.

Chapter 5: What We Have Is Good for Us; What They Have Is Good for Them

Another way to relate to people of other religions is to practice mutual indifference. This means that we should simply leave each other alone, and thus avoid conflict and allow people to develop into better religious persons within their own traditions.

1. What are the ways in which our treatment of religion as an individual and private matter influences the manner in which we relate to people of other religions?

2. What are the areas in the life of your town, city, state, or nation that require people of different religions to work together? Have you participated in any programs that call for such a working together?

Chapter 6: We Know in Full; They Know in Part

While appreciating the truth and goodness in other religions, Christians may see them as partial and lacking in fullness. According to this view, people of other religions are engaged in a quest which can be satisfied only by the Christian faith.

1. In what ways does our perception of other religions as unfulfilled quests affect the way we relate to the people of those religious traditions? Are there times when you find that your own spiritual journey appears to be an unfulfilled quest?

2. How would you characterize the spirituality of persons of other religions whom you know or read about? In what ways may one find life to be more than an unfulfilled quest?

Chapter 7: We Know and Know That We Know; They Know and Know Not That They Know

Since Christ is the Word (Logos) that enlightens every human being, one could relate to people of other religions as those who are guided by Christ in their journey toward God, though they do not name that as Christ.

1. What are the ways in which this approach enables you to accept and appreciate the people of other religions? What are the difficulties that you may experience in this approach?

2. Are there phrases, words, or images that you may use to express the idea behind the phrase "anonymous Christian"?

Chapter 8: We and They Together
Need to Know More!

Knowing that we and they are distinct but interconnected, one may approach the people of other religions as partners in a dialogue that leads to mutual edification, spiritual growth, and joint action for justice and peace.

1. Invite a person of another religious tradition (Jewish, Hindu, Muslim, or other) to share with you his or her experience of God and God's grace in his or her life. Following the presentation you may actually engage in a conversation with the guest regarding questions such as (a) What are the liturgical and ritualistic practices in one another's religious tradition that we find helpful in times of pain and sorrow? (b) What impels us toward love and compassion?

2. If you are not able to invite a person, you may discuss the following two questions: (a) What are the conversations that you have engaged with persons of other religions? What are the insights that you bring from those conversations for understanding the nature of dialogue? (b) What are the ways in which one may find conversation to be a genuine form of witness or just a "warm up" for actual witnessing?

Chapter 9: Gentleness and Reverence

We are called upon to bear witness to the love of God which we have come to see in the face of Jesus the Christ. Such a witness demands from us a deep sensitivity to the movement of the Spirit of God among the people of other religions, and a willingness to practice "gentleness" and "reverence" in the process of witnessing.

1. How would you have responded to Sundar and Sita if they had come to you with the kind of questions they had? Are there ways to respond other than what the author did?

2. What are the practical ways in which we and the people in our churches may practice gentleness and reverence?

CPSIA information can be obtained at www.ICGtesting.com
Printed in the USA
LVOW13s2006110814

398588LV00018B/895/P